PRAISE FOR
A DOG NAMED MATTIS

"When I lived in Atlanta, Mark Tappan was my favorite neighbor! His love for his family, his career, and his community was infectious. You can imagine my delight when I saw him start sharing his story online with the world. That excitement doubled when he sent me his new book! You are going to love meeting Mattis inside these pages!"

— Jon Acuff, *New York Times* bestselling
author of *Soundtracks*

"It is something special to know Mark and Mattis, and it's no surprise why so many people are drawn to their close relationship. This book brings readers on an intimate ride-along of Mark and Mattis's journey together. Mark shares the important life lessons that he has learned from his brave K9 companion, Mattis, with a message of trust, service, and community that is so vitally needed in the world right now. You won't be able to put the book down, and it will impact the way you view the courageous humans and K9s in law enforcement."

— Katie Linendoll, tech influencer, TV personality,
and country music artist

"Mark and Mattis have a bond unlike any I've seen between a man and his dog. Most officers and their K9 partners have undeniable bonds. They have to; oftentimes the job they are doing together could be life or death. But when I first met (and interviewed) Mark, I could see the love and adoration he had for Mattis; in fact, he cried just talking about his dog. This book takes you on their journey together, realizing and exceeding the true meaning behind 'man's best friend.' There's no doubt that after reading

about this incredible German shepherd, as a heralded K9 officer and as a dog at home, you'll fall in love just as I did. They are a dynamic duo and the people of Alpharetta, Georgia, are lucky to have been protected by them. May we all aspire to love and respect our dogs like Mark does."

—Jamie Little, FOX sports broadcaster for Motorsports
and the Westminster Kennel Club Dog Show

"Inspirational, instructional, and best of all heartwarming. Mark and Mattis take the reader on a journey into a variety of moments that provide vital life lessons for any canine handler or dog enthusiast. Dense educational content paired with raw experience, this book is capturing the tenacity and passion in canine partnership."

—Sara Carson, celebrity dog trainer

A DOG NAMED
MATTIS

A DOG NAMED
MATTIS

12 LESSONS FOR LIVING COURAGEOUSLY, SERVING SELFLESSLY, AND BUILDING BRIDGES FROM A HEROIC K9 OFFICER

MARK TAPPAN

NELSON BOOKS

An Imprint of Thomas Nelson

A Dog Named Mattis

Published in Nashville, Tennessee, by Nelson Books, an imprint of Thomas Nelson. Nelson Books and Thomas Nelson are registered trademarks of HarperCollins Christian Publishing, Inc.

The author is represented by Alive Literary Agency, www.aliveliterary.com.

Thomas Nelson titles may be purchased in bulk for educational, business, fundraising, or sales promotional use. For information, please email SpecialMarkets@ThomasNelson.com.

Library of Congress Cataloging-in-Publication Data

Names: Tappan, Mark, 1974- author.
Title: A dog named Mattis : 12 lessons for living courageously, serving selflessly, and building bridges from a heroic K9 officer / Mark Tappan.
Description: Nashville, Tennessee : Nelson Books, [2024] | Summary: "Sergeant Mark Tappan shares the twelve lessons he's learned from his amazing K9 partner Mattis, whose heroic actions will remind readers to live courageously, serve selflessly, and love passionately because every human (and dog) has a purpose"-- Provided by publisher.
Identifiers: LCCN 2023055148 (print) | LCCN 2023055149 (ebook) | ISBN 9781400246687 (tp) | ISBN 9781400246656 (epub)
Subjects: LCSH: Tappan, Mark, 1974- | Police dogs--United States. | Police--United States--Biography. | Human-animal relationships—United States. | Human-animal relationships--Religious aspects--Christianity.
Classification: LCC HV8025 .T368 2024 (print) | LCC HV8025 (ebook) | DDC 363.2--dc23/eng/20240124
LC record available at https://lccn.loc.gov/2023055148
LC ebook record available at https://lccn.loc.gov/2023055149

Printed in the United States of America

24 25 26 27 28 LBC 5 4 3 2 1

I dedicate this to the Marine Corps, who led an irresponsible boy down a path to become a man, and to the most inspirational marine in my life, Uncle Marcus. Semper Fi!

CONTENTS

GO ALL IN

*Whatever you do, work at it with
all your heart, as working for the
Lord, not for human masters.*
—COLOSSIANS 3:23

Some moments change your life forever. You don't know that's the case at the time, and these moments are almost always unexpected. The impact they will have on your future is unpredictable.

In Pursuit

I gave a description of the fleeing vehicle over the radio: a silver BMW passenger car with Florida tags, driven by two males. Last seen heading north on Georgia 400 from Haynes Bridge Road. Traffic was thick, as it always was around 5 p.m. on a weekday. The only thing I knew was that the car had hastily blown through a red light when I pulled in behind it and was nimbler and accelerated faster than my Chevy Tahoe police cruiser. Plus, unlike most police cruisers, the entirety of my back seat was a kennel—metal frame, rubber mat, and a "spill-proof" water bowl—with some important cargo: Mattis.

I also knew the driver of the BMW was willing to put other people's lives at risk by the way they were driving through heavy traffic: blasting through red lights (which was the original reason I attempted to stop them), excessive speed (about ninety miles per hour in a forty-five), and weaving in and out of lanes, almost striking dozens of drivers who were just trying to get home. When you're in this position as a police officer, you have to weigh the necessity to apprehend against the potential danger of a pursuit. Typically, the truth is, if someone runs, there is more to the story than what the initial stop was for, but you as an officer are scrutinized based on what you knew at the time you decided whether to pursue. I made it clear: "Radio, I am terminating pursuit."

I shut down my flashing blue lights and sirens and reduced my speed, but I continued in the direction the fleeing vehicle was headed. Few cars and fewer drivers are made to handle the type of driving the driver of the BMW was engaging in.

There is a feeling of failure when you call off a pursuit, like the air leaking out of a balloon. A majority of law enforcement work—I'd say probably 99 percent—deals with the mundane, so when chaos makes an appearance, you feel your blood warm, your eyes widen, and fulfillment set in. You spend hours training for the chaos, and you spend even more time running through chaotic scenarios in your head. I got into law enforcement to find the bad guys, chase them if need be, and protect my community. Ironically, the last part—protection—is the reason I needed to shut down this particular chase.

Your mind wanders in moments like these, and you find yourself asking, Who were they (the tag came back to a rental vehicle, a common way criminals conceal their identity when traveling to commit crimes), what did they do (besides run a red light), and where might they be headed (usually they would head toward the freeway for a quick escape)?

Another officer who had wisely placed himself north of my location in a parking lot next to a busy intersection suddenly broadcasted, "Radio, I have a silver BMW, Florida tag, with two males that just wrecked out at Old Milton Parkway and North Point Parkway. [What did I tell you? Most drivers aren't able to handle the type of driving they were engaging in.] One male is headed north, one is headed south across Old Milton Parkway."

Another unit chimed in that they were headed to the area. They were a veteran squad so they each knew the tasks that needed to happen: secure the vehicle and contain the area because a K9 unit—Mattis and I—was close.

I looked over my shoulder and told Mattis, "We're back in this!" I activated the lights and set the siren wailing again.

I had to choose quickly which direction to go, north or south. The north location already had two units on scene, and south had no one. It was also easier for me to get to and might increase the chances of cutting off the fleeing suspect. Plus, I had a vague familiarity with the woods behind the shopping center, which backed up to Big Creek.

South it was. I turned south on North Point Parkway, then made a quick turn into the strip mall on the corner of Old Milton and North Point. There was a passageway behind the businesses and a retaining wall with a decent drop-off on the other side leading down to a creek. The suspect would have no choice but to run right to where I was waiting. I threw the Tahoe into Park, jumped out, and ran to the corner of the building to ensure he would have limited options for escape.

K9 police vehicles are designed with what I call a door popper. It's a tiny remote box on my duty belt with a button. You hit the button and the passenger-side K9 door flies open. I had trained Mattis that when that door opened, he needed to run and find me as quickly as possible. I wanted the "Mattis deterrent" with me in this foot chase. I figured if the suspect saw one hundred pounds of determination and teeth headed toward him, he might be encouraged to peacefully surrender.

There is a slight delay between when the button is pushed and when the door opens (maybe two seconds), and in that time I spotted the suspect coming from behind the businesses. Training took over. I gave location and told dispatch I had the suspect on foot. Utter shock showed on his face when he saw Mattis and me. I shouted for him to get on the ground as I continued to run toward him. I meant the ground in front of him, but he chose the ground on the other side of the retaining wall. He leapt over the metal guardrail that was just above the retaining wall, determined to continue his escape.

In some places, the retaining wall drop-off to below was about ten feet. I was mentally prepared to make that jump (fall, really) and knew Mattis could too. He jumped off high obstacles with ease, and the descent was never an issue. The more complicated issue was how my forty-one-year-old body would handle the descent. Tuck and roll and I would be fine . . . ish. I hopped the guardrail. That's when my decision-making process encountered a hiccup. The suspect was still falling. What I thought was ten feet was more like thirty feet. Standing on the cobblestone brick that lined the retaining wall, momentum propelling me forward, I grasped the metal guardrail with my right hand as my feet slipped off, and I hung there.

Mattis had caught up, and he did exactly what he was supposed to do when that door flies open: find his best friend and run next to him. He started his jump two feet before the guardrail and gracefully cleared it with ease. That moment in time is carved into my memory, and as I reflect now, it still feels like it lasted an eternity. I could see that Mattis had also processed his landing, and I saw something in his expression I had never seen before: fear.

His body hunched and seemingly frozen, he glanced at me as if he hoped I could save him somehow.

There was absolutely nothing I could do as I watched him fall through the air. I had put him in this situation, he had trusted me implicitly, and I had possibly led him to his demise. I pleaded internally, *Please, Lord, let him be okay! Please, Lord!* I pulled myself back onto the wall.

The suspect hit the ground on his feet, jamming his knees to his chest. Mattis was precise in his calculations and landed right on top of the suspect's shoulders. He tumbled and rolled about five feet away from the suspect and glanced up at me for further instruction. You see, through it all, he was on a "run next to me" command, not an apprehend (bite) command. I pulled myself back onto the ledge and tried to compose my thoughts. *"Auf!"* I commanded, giving Mattis the Dutch command (the language he was trained in) to lie down.

"Lay down, you move, and you are going to get bit!" This command was for the suspect, letting him know the means to a peaceful outcome. I motioned from thirty feet above for Mattis to get closer to the suspect to encourage good decisions from the man.

I had to figure out how to get down there, but I was panicking. I was concerned for Mattis. I wanted to just fling myself down the wall, but I knew that the combination of my gear and the distance I would fall would lead to bones exploding on impact.

As I looked around, I noticed a tree about five feet away from the retaining wall. I'm no arborist but I would describe it as an oak. I considered jumping to it and sliding down. But I was wearing an outer vest carrier with a medical pack, magazine pouches, and handcuffs, which would prevent me from hugging the tree to my chest as I slid down. The tree had no limbs; in fact, I could see that it had recently been trimmed so that branches wouldn't interfere with the integrity of the retaining wall. The tree was out.

I could break visual contact and look for a way to get down there, but that would mean losing control over Mattis and possibly allowing the suspect to take off. I also didn't know whether the suspect was armed, and if he was, I was taking a chance that the second I disappeared from view, my partner could be hurt.

I felt an overwhelming sense of helplessness. I couldn't come up with a solution. But then I heard the screeching tires of another officer pulling into the parking lot. Finally, a solution. As the officer got out of the vehicle and ran toward me, I started barking orders. "I need you to find a way down there and get that guy in custody!" Without hesitation, he did what I couldn't do in the moment. He looked around and found a route down to where they were. He ran back toward North Point Parkway, down the sidewalk, and cut back into the woods by the creek.

I waited above and shouted encouragement to my dog—"Good boy, Mattis, watch him!"—and discouragement to the suspect: "Don't you move!" The captain came into my vision. He seemed surprised to see Mattis down there. He looked up at me and asked, "What do you want me to do?"

"Put him in cuffs!"

"What about Mattis?" I could tell he was apprehensive about approaching the suspect because he worried Mattis might go for the first thing that moved.

"You will be fine!" (I already knew Mattis was the goodest boy!)

As soon as I heard the distinct sound of the cuffs catching, I sprinted toward my dog, following the same route the other officer had taken.

As I approached Mattis, I unlatched the three-foot leash I kept around my waist and slid on my knees through the dead October leaves. I did what I was trained to do and checked his structural frame. I ran my hand down his back, each of his limbs, his ribs, and his tail to see whether he would react. Nothing, not even a whimper. I grabbed his massive head and pulled it to mine and hugged him. Before getting to relax in the satisfaction that my brief prayer as he was falling over the wall had been answered, I heard on the radio, "293 [my badge number], is your partner available to help with the other suspect?"

I looked at the other officer. "You good here?"

"Yep, go."

"293, I'm en route. Where do you need me?"

"North side of Old Milton, in the woods by the west side of the creek."

"All right, buddy, we are not done yet!" I told Mattis as I loaded him into the Tahoe. Lights, sirens, and we were at the other location in less than a minute. A perimeter officer pointed in the direction as I got Mattis out and hooked him up to his short leash. We ran in the direction the officer had pointed.

We covered ground quickly, mostly because Mattis knew exactly what to do, without any command. He dragged me in the direction of the second suspect at a full sprint. It was all I could do to hold on to the leash. We flew by the other officers who were in chase.

Up ahead I saw the second suspect running up—or attempting to run up—a steep embankment covered with dried leaves. For every foot he gained, he would slip back another two. Capture was imminent, and he knew it. He looked back and saw Mattis closing in, managing to maintain traction even with the leaves, and he knew he was caught. He wisely threw up his hands and surrendered with a heavy sigh. Other officers stepped in and took him into custody.

Before the satisfaction of accomplishment could set in, I heard a single whimper, and then Mattis collapsed with a heavy thud and crackle of dried leaves.

In that moment, my heart broke and I berated myself.

Why did you hit that door popper?

You should have leashed him up!

Will he make it?

Will he be able to return as my partner?

I gathered him up off the ground, and again he whimpered in pain. I whispered as I carried him the two hundred yards back to the Tahoe, "You're going to be okay, bud!" mixed with audible prayers of "Please let him be okay, Lord!" I laid him down in his kennel, got into the car, and keyed up my in-car radio. "Dispatch, notify the emergency vet I'm en route and my partner is hurt. Tell them to get ready." I knew time was the enemy. Lights, sirens . . . I don't remember the length of time it took to get there, but I do remember pleading for traffic to get out of the way and begging God for the life of my best friend.

With All Your Heart

When I first got into dog training, my dad told me, "Remember, son, all that dog wants to do is make you happy." There were no truer words than those for Mattis. He did things with total focus, with all his strength and all his heart, because he trusted me and wanted to make me happy.

Years before I got into police K9 work, when I was a youth pastor at a church in Southern California, I remember setting up chairs before youth group. It was a menial task that I thought interfered with the more important things. The senior pastor of the church must have detected my lack of enthusiasm for the chore. One day he started helping me, then he looked over at me and said, "We need to make sure these are perfect, as if you were setting them up because Jesus was coming to youth group tonight."

His words were simple but they had a profound impact on me. From that moment on, Colossians 3:23 became one of my favorite verses. "*Whatever* you do, work at it with all your heart, as if working for the Lord, not for human masters" (emphasis added).

Years later, when I started working with Mattis, I discovered that he lived out that verse. Every moment I spent with him—from the very day I selected him—he did everything with all his heart.

Dogs are special, and Mattis is the most special one I have ever known.

BUILD BRIDGES, NOT WALLS

*"By this everyone will know that you are
my disciples, if you love one another."*
—JOHN 13:35

Dogs build bridges where there are no roads.

Interacting with the Community

Before law enforcement and youth ministry work, I served as a marine. If you had asked me my plan when I enlisted, it would have been to go straight from the Marine Corps into law enforcement. God had different plans. He was still preparing me to be a police officer (I truly believe I was called to be in law enforcement), but I was lacking in certain areas—namely, empathy and compassion. So he shook my world up and taught me the value of people for ten years. In my time as a youth pastor I learned to consider people as image bearers of God. That season also helped me see that we are all flawed and need Jesus, and it reminded me of all the grace I had been shown in my life. This was a good starting point for my next career.

I entered law enforcement in 2006. Almost from the start I saw a shift in the way that our profession was received by the public. Incident after incident would make the news and drive a wedge between our society and law enforcement. In his 9 Policing Principles, Sir Robert Peel wrote,

"To recognize always that the power of the police to fulfill their functions and duties is dependent on public approval of their existence, actions, and behavior, and on their ability to secure and maintain public respect."

I believe this wholeheartedly. In my career I have made it a goal to be open and honest, to carry out my job with honor in order to build a bridge where a wedge is being driven. However, politicians, the media, and our own poor behaviors are driving law enforcement and the public further apart. Because of that, I make it a point to volunteer for community service events and demonstrations. I want to do whatever I can to mend relationships.

Very early in my law enforcement career I tried out for and made the department's special weapons and tactics (SWAT) team. This assignment was in addition to my normal patrol assignment. I loved the challenge and training and the community events we got to participate in. In the summer of 2012, I was excited to show off our department's new SWAT command vehicle at the Touch-a-Truck event. Up until then, our SWAT team had rolled around in a reclaimed county school bus. They had repainted it black and written SWAT in white letters on both sides. Unfortunately, they hadn't removed the old letters before painting the bus, so you could still read Fulton County Schools on both sides. The seats were made for teenagers, not fully grown men decked out in SWAT kits. It was like watching a slapstick comedy every time we got on the bus, got off the bus, and tried to maneuver inside.

This new vehicle, though, was perfect. It was custom-made to our needs. It had cushioned bench seating on each side with a spacious aisle in the center and exits at both the rear and side. It had a mobile dispatch command terminal in the front and storage to carry all of our fancy equipment: shields, night vision goggles, breaching equipment, flash-bangs, smoke grenades, robots, and cameras. It also had an exterior monitor that our commander could hook his computer up to for going over operational plans. Our city was proud of the vehicle as well since all the funding came from seized drug money. We called it Black Beauty, and I could not wait to show it off at Touch-a-Truck.

I loved doing these events because I valued community support and approval of what we do. Opportunities to show off impressive gear and interact are crucial for that. Plus, the park was close to my house, so my own kids could come. I held on to the hope that my nine-year-old daughter and six-year-old son might think their dad was cool.

Fresh from the car wash, we arrived at the event early to set up a display. The event coordinator told us we would be the first vehicle people saw when they entered. We brought folding tables on which to set up our most impressive gear, like a sniper rifle painted in camo with a bipod. (The firing mechanism was removed to make it safe.) There was one of our brand-new rifles all the team carried with a collapsible stock, shortened barrel, and special targeting scopes with lights built in and suppressors that made it shoot more quietly (and also made it safe). We had some of the tools we use to open doors forcefully, like a ram and a Halligan pry bar. There was a 40 mm grenade launcher that we used to launch

- CS gas (tear gas) into a structure that makes you cough and tear up uncontrollably;
- large foam bullets that hurt really bad but don't do permanent damage;
- smoke to conceal our location; and
- illumination grenades to light up a scene we need to see better.

There was a station where kids and adults could try on a SWAT vest and helmet to feel the weight we must carry around. (All the gear together weighed about forty pounds.) They could also throw on a sniper ghillie suit, a suit that basically looks like a swamp monster. We had music pumping through Black Beauty's external speakers, stickers for all the kiddos, and shade since the command vehicle had an attached awning that extended from one side.

Finally, we had great stories with which to entertain the masses:

- The time we had to search a house for kidnapping suspects at 2 a.m. We snuck up to the door, rammed it until it flew open, then threw in a flash-bang grenade (loud noise, big flash of light to distract, no physical damage), but it hit the door that was swinging closed and landed at my feet while half the team took off. My buddy and I stayed put, it exploded, we went in, and there we saw a very large woman who lacked clothing screaming. She took off running down the hall. We saw a couple of guns lying around, so we went after her. She tripped and fell, and my buddy fell right on top of her. We put her in handcuffs, sat her up, and gave her a blanket. Next thing we heard was the oven timer dinging. Lobster and butter sauce were in the oven. Who cooks lobster at 2 a.m.?!

- There was the time we were called in for a statewide manhunt for two guys who had killed a law enforcement officer. We drove an hour in our brand-new command vehicle with lights and sirens blazing. We learned it wasn't really made to go fast down bumpy country dirt roads. Gear and people were flying around in the back. We were working alongside local municipalities and federal agencies who were coordinating the hunt around a huge wooded area by a lake. The federal agent in charge of directing our group guided us the wrong way, but we ended up locating the suspects and taking them into custody peacefully.

- And then there were the SWAT competitions we went to, which were composed of hostage-rescue scenarios, active-shooter scenarios, shooting accuracy and speed drills, obstacle courses, and sniper challenges.

Everything was set up perfectly and we were ready for the crowds. Oddly, there was an empty space for a display between us and the other display, a traffic unit with shiny motorcycles. I asked the event coordinator who was supposed to be there, and she told me the K9 unit. I made some calls, but no one knew who was signed up to fill the spot. I explained it was possible they had gotten busy on a call and would make it when they could.

We had it all, and as the crowds began showing up, they flocked to our display. (Except my kids. They seemed to enjoy the garbage truck more.) Moms, dads, kids, and grandparents were thoroughly enjoying the music, the stories, the equipment, and the shade (it was a hot day)! This was the perfect setting, and I was loving it. Kids and parents were trying on gear, asking great questions, and belly laughing at our stories. As people left our station, we saw them pointing back, telling other event-goers they needed to make the trip over to SWAT land.

About an hour into the event, a dirty Chevy Impala approached the empty display spot. It was black and white with extremely dark tinted windows, and it had red lettering on both sides and the back that said K9 Unit. We lifted the tape and the vehicle pulled into the space. Then I saw something that would change my future and have a serious impact on my life: the interaction between the crowd and the K9.

As soon as that K9 team showed up, the crowds around our display began to dwindle. And it wasn't just our display that was experiencing this but every display at the event. People are always drawn to dogs. The officer had nothing prepared, just an amazing creature that did a job everyone was fascinated by. Onlookers had endless questions for the handler and cheered at anything the dog performed. You could see the genuine interest on every person's face as they hung on every word and every trick. At our display, we would be in the middle of showing something to someone when suddenly they would notice the dog and leave our station in a trance, headed straight for the K9 unit.

As I watched, a seed was planted that continued to be cultivated over the next couple of years of my career. The more I learned, the more I was drawn toward the K9 unit. It attracted me for three reasons:

1. **The challenge.** We had some handlers who took great pride in their job, and it showed in the quality of work they put out. I saw in them a high level of commitment. Their job didn't stop when mine did. They took the dogs home with them and cared for them every hour of every day. They were training constantly—even more than SWAT—to maintain their skills. They were doing demonstrations daily. I saw it as the ultimate challenge in law enforcement, and I wanted to be a part of it.

2. **The way people responded to dogs and the opportunity to make the most of it.** In the tumultuous cultural environment we were navigating, we had this bridge in K9s that could heal, if we would only use it well. I wanted to focus on the community relations aspect as much as being a great handler.

3. **My absolute love for dogs.** My dad field trained labs when I was growing up, so my whole life I was surrounded by intelligent dogs that could assist people. I was in awe of how the dogs intently focused on my dad's every motion, word, and blow of the dog whistle. He and the dogs had this amazing connection. The best thing about dogs, though, is not their ability to perform tasks but their capacity to be loyal friends. It is what really sets them apart from any other animal. They usually have one human that is theirs. Growing up, I was my dog Sylvester's human. He was a tiny but fierce twenty-five-pound white spitz. My dad said he was untrainable, but Sylvester listened to me. I can't tell you the hours I spent unloading teenage-boy concerns on him. He would pant, smile, and just want to play more, making the concerns disappear.

I had only one goal for my career after that day at the Touch-a-Truck event and it was to be in the K9 unit, but it's difficult to get onto the team, in part because there are seldom any openings. In the law enforcement world, when you become a handler, you are making a commitment to be that dog's handler for the span of his service, which could be anywhere from six to ten years. Then, once that dog's service is up, you have the choice to stay in the unit and handle another dog, which the majority of handlers do, or go back to patrol work.

There is something you should know about me. My mother instilled in me a belief that I could do anything if I worked hard enough. "You have two arms and two legs just like anybody else. There's no reason you can't!" she would say. I always believed her, and her words were in my mind as I set my sights on what I wanted to do: I would be the department's next handler.

Tryouts

In December 2012 I found out that the handler of Niko, a four-year-old midsize German shepherd, was retiring and the department was looking for a new handler. I knew and loved Niko. He had a bit of an attitude problem, but who was I to judge?

The head of the K9 unit put out an email detailing the requirements for the job. They wanted an officer with at least two years of experience in law enforcement, a letter from a supervisor, two examples of reports of crimes the officer had composed, and the ability to pass the physical test and compete in an interview board. The email also explained that the physical test requirements could be found in departmental policy, and the interview questions would come from departmental policy, state law, and established case law.

I had almost seven years of experience, so I was covered there. Next, rather than get a letter from one supervisor, I got a letter from every supervisor I had ever worked for. For examples of report writing, I provided cases that showed I was willing to take extra investigative steps in areas where a K9 could be utilized. But I also did something I figured no one else putting in for the position would do: I included a report that was poor along with a memo explaining that I didn't just want to highlight my best but also something I did poorly and what I learned from it. I took all of that paperwork, made five copies (one for each person who would be selecting the next handler), and had it bound with a cover sheet and laminated. I wanted to show how badly I desired this position.

The physical test consisted of a mile-and-a-half run that had to be completed in under thirteen minutes; a hundred-yard carry of an eighty-pound K9 in under forty seconds; and lifting an eighty-pound K9 over a five-foot wall. Now, the hundred-yard K9 carry and wall lift probably don't sound that difficult, especially since I had spent the last six years of my career on the SWAT team, which had exceptionally high physical standards. I had won the past two top SWAT competitions at the Georgia Tactical Officers Association annual training. I could run a mile in full SWAT kit in under seven minutes. This would be an absolute piece of cake, right? What you have to remember, though, is that the dog is not your K9, and in general, police K9s do not like to be carried by people they don't know. In fact, they get downright angry—fighting angry!

For the interview portion, I studied a lot. I made sure

I knew departmental policy inside and out. I found every major court case involving the use of K9s in every discipline they are used for: narcotics detection, tracking, apprehension, and article searches. I was more prepared for this test than any other test or interview I had ever encountered in my life.

The day of the tryouts arrived. We were told to meet behind the Alpharetta Community Center for the physical test. This was also the first time I would get to see who my competition was. I'd heard rumors about who might put in, but up until that day I didn't know for sure. There were some excellent candidates—six, including myself and one former K9 handler. I thought for sure he had the advantage since he had been through this process before. He would know exactly what questions would be asked and what he needed to do to be selected. In fact, he had even sat on selection committees before, which meant he understood the grading criteria.

I wasn't nervous about any of this, though. My mindset was that I had worked hard throughout my career to demonstrate who I was. I had prepared thoroughly for this moment. I was going to give my absolute best and hoped the other candidates would as well. At the end of the day, if they didn't select me, it meant I wasn't the right candidate. My goal wasn't to beat everyone else, just to clearly show who I was. (But I really wanted to win.)

First event: the mile-and-a-half run. All of the candidates were stretching in a group and discussing what was to come. Whenever someone shared a concern, the rest of the group would offer some encouragement that they could overcome it. I shared a genuine concern I had. I had recently started to experience pain in my lower abdomen. It kept me from going all out on a sprint, and I knew that when I was carrying one of the K9s, I would have to engage my core and move pretty fast to make the time. (It was undiagnosed at the time, but later I found out I had a tear in my abdomen wall. More about this in a later lesson.) All of the guys offered encouragement, but later I learned that sharing that concern almost cost me my dream job.

Finally, it was time to line up for the first portion. All of the active K9 handlers were there to watch, and the commander of the unit was actually running with us. We were told time really didn't matter and that it was just pass or fail. That did not compute for me. They would get my all-out effort. My body type really wasn't built for distance running (I have short legs), but I was decent at pushing myself, and I was first across the finish line in under ten minutes. One of the candidates began cramping and was unable to finish. It was disheartening because he was a good guy and very intelligent. Everyone else made the time.

Next up was the K9 carry. The handler of the dog I was going to carry walked over to his SUV and opened the door to the kennel. As he did, a billowing cloud of fur floated from the kennel. I remember thinking, *If my wife saw that, she would never let me be a K9 handler!* The handler placed a hard, riveted leather muzzle on his dog, whose name was Lekso.

Fun fact that I learned later: dogs are ritualistic learners. What that meant in this case was that every time the trainer went through the ritual of putting a muzzle on Lekso, the dog knew he was about to do apprehension training. He would not be able to use his teeth but would instead do something called a muzzle punch: driving the hard, riveted leather muzzle into whatever he was trying to apprehend. Lekso knew, because he was a smart dog, that wearing the muzzle meant it was fight time.

This is a fun fact because what do you think Lekso began to do to my face when I leaned down to pick him up? *Ding, ding, ding!* Muzzle punch time. Some of the other candidates took their time and tried to avoid the swinging and stabbing of the angry German shepherd's head. My strategy was to get hit a few times on the way down to lift him up, then hold him close and tuck my head. *Whap, whap* to the left temple area. It made me a little dizzy but I was fine. The real concern was the pain in my abdomen. This part was definitely the biggest physical challenge for me. When a dog is flailing, you have to really engage your core to hold him tight. I pushed through and made the time, but a sharp, searing pain tore through the lower left side of my abdomen. I carefully lowered Lekso to the ground and tried to give him a little scratch as a thank-you. He returned the gesture by attempting another muzzle punch.

Next was the wall lift. Not really that hard a test for most of the candidates of an average height, but being five foot six meant I had to stand on my tippy-toes and stretch my abdomen a bit. It hurt, of course, but I managed. Up and over the wall Lekso went into the loving arms of his handler, with a few muzzle punches along the way for encouragement. Thank you, Lekso.

The interview portion was the last part of the process. Since I finished first in the mile and a half, I got to choose the order in which the interviews were conducted. I chose to go first. We met at a city building just down the road from the park where the tests were conducted. I don't remember being nervous at all; I was just excited for the opportunity. I walked in and slid the laminated booklets of recommendations, cases, and my résumé over to each of the board members. I felt prepared for each of the questions. I had a passion about the subject because of my fascination with what K9 teams did, and I really hoped that it showed. It didn't feel like some interviews, where I was just trying to regurgitate information I had memorized. When the interview was over, I walked out feeling confident, not that I would win but that I had done my best. I drove home thanking God for that.

Now I had to wait. I hate waiting. I did the math in my head of how long it should take them to make a decision. My interview took about twenty minutes, and there were four more candidates to go, so that was an hour and twenty minutes. But you need to build in some breaks between interviews for the board, and you can't forget to add in the time needed for discussion. So maybe it would take around two hours for them to decide, then they would have to contact the chief of police and let him know of their decision and see whether he approved.

My phone rang two hours after I left the interview room. It was the commander of the unit. That was fast.

Him: Hey, Mark. How do you feel you did?
Me: I truly feel like I did my best, so I am very content with that.
Him: We had some really good candidates.
Me: I agree. I was happy to compete against them.
Him: We had to consider not only who did the best but who would be the best match for Niko.
Me: I understand.

(This phone call was beginning to feel like what Ryan Seacrest does at the end of every *American Idol*: "The votes are in, and after a nationwide vote, I'm sorry to say, but . . . you are going to have to wait until after the commercial break!")

Him: Well, unfortunately . . .
Me: . . .
Him: you're going to have to take time away from your family because you are our next *American Idol*—whoops, K9 handler!
Me: Thank you, sir. I promise I won't let you down and you will get my very best!

A New Handler for Niko

Some moments don't seem big enough to hold the emotions that overwhelm you in an instant. This was a moment like that. Time is a constant, but too many things were happening at once as I hung up the phone. Part of me knew my life was about to change forever, but I also knew I had no idea to what extent. To say that I was ecstatic would be accurate but barely adequate to capture all the emotions I was feeling.

Some new emotions arose when I got my next phone call, this time from the deputy director. He told me not to be concerned but he had received a letter from one of the candidates saying I was unfit to be a K9 handler. Because I had a medical concern in my abdomen, the candidate thought a K9 handler's course would be too arduous for me to handle. The deputy director said he thought I should know what someone was saying behind my back. I was hurt they would betray my trust, and I was angry.

I had to focus, though; I knew there would always be people who would try to bring me down. I now had the opportunity to meet the greatest challenge I would ever have in police work, and hopefully I would do it with excellence. Further, becoming a K9 handler would provide an avenue not only to do my job better but also to build a bridge with the community. It was now time to try to bond with Niko—who I was a little scared of.

PRIDE IS THE ENEMY

"For those who exalt themselves will be humbled."
—MATTHEW 23:12

The SWAT commander once called me the most com- petitive person he ever met. If I like something, I want to be the best ever. A quote from a baseball movie, *The Natural*, sums up how I approach endeavors I have a passion for. When the main character, Roy Hobbs, is asked what he hopes to accomplish, he answers, "When I walk down the street, people would have looked and they would have said, 'There goes Roy Hobbs, the best there ever was in this game.'" In the movie he wanted every record, he wanted to do things that had never been done before, and he wanted to leave no doubt in the minds of anyone who knew about him that he was the best. To this day it is still one of my favorite movies because I feel that current of desire to do the most I possibly can with what I've been given, to strive for a level of excellence that has never been obtained.

Growing up, I practiced martial arts. I held numerous state titles, regional titles, national championships, and two world championships. I once showed up for the national championship tournament after not competing or training for over a year (because of my enlistment in the Marine Corps) and won. In the Marine Corps there is a regular promotional cycle, and occasionally they have competitions for meritorious promotions among your battalion (up to 1,200 marines). Battalion commanders look at your fitness scores and evaluations and test your knowledge in a formal interview board. I received two meritorious promotions in my four years, which was a very uncommon feat. I held records in sit-ups and shooting in boot camp. In the police academy I won the highest award, the Director's Award, for the most outstanding recruit in character and leadership. I made the department's SWAT team in under two years on my first try. I won two state top SWAT operator's titles, which was an event consisting of shooting accuracy, a distance run, and an obstacle course for time.

I was not only competitive and driven but also proud of those accomplishments and the work it had taken to achieve them. But the Bible says pride comes before a fall, and my fall was coming. I was about to learn that I knew nothing about working as a police K9 handler, and if I was going to become a good handler, I would have to learn to trust a dog who knew more than I did.

Trust Your Dog

On day one of my handler's course in Maysville, Georgia, I saw Niko for the first time as "my dog." I had seen him at work with his previous handler, but this was different. Up till now, I had watched him from a distance with a reverent respect, almost fear. Now we were supposed to be a team.

Niko was a dark, sable-colored, seventy-five-pound German shepherd. I was told to brush him out to start to build a bond with him. He was freshly bathed and still slightly wet. I felt a bit apprehensive because I had seen the extremely aggressive side of working dogs toward people they don't know (Lekso taught me this lesson), and Niko was not muzzled. As I ran the shedding brush along his side, wicking away the excess water, all the accomplishments, all the promotions, awards, and accolades that I had meant nothing to Niko. I was about to learn the most valuable lesson you can learn as a handler: trust your dog.

Every time I screwed up in training, I knew what phrase I was going to hear from one of the instructors. And I heard it often. I guarantee it is the most uttered phrase at every handler school across the country. You see, we use dogs because of their ability to smell. We are asking them to do what we cannot do, and as the handlers we must understand what they are trying to communicate. New handlers often miss the message the dog is trying to communicate and rely on what they think they know in their own minds. The result is that you miss the track or the odor the dog is finding.

Niko was a four-year-old that already had two years of experience in the field with a seasoned handler. He was the expert, and I was not. The instructors knew this, Niko knew this, and the key to this handler's course was teaching me to learn to rely on my expert partner and not myself.

Every day of the first month began the same way: kennel

maintenance. I am not sure if it is a conscious effort to teach you your place in the relationship with your dog or just a practical one because you have to learn to care for your dog. Looking back, I see that it accomplished both. The school where I was training had covered outdoor kennels with chain-link fences and concrete floors. Overnight, the high-energy working dogs make quite the mess of these kennels. On the first day, I wore non-waterproof tennis shoes. That was the last day I made that mistake; every day after that I wore waterproof boots. I don't gag easily, but the smell of those kennels is forever etched into my memory. I actually still remember the odor of the bio-friendly industrial-strength disinfectant spray we cleaned with. The message I received was clear: You are the one who cleans up after him. He is the important one.

Day after day Niko would remind me of that as well. He would nail whatever the task was, I would misread, and the instructor would yell, "Mark, trust your dog!" Sometimes the instructor would decorate the phrase with expletives to emphasize its importance. Slowly, more and more, I would learn that the key to being a good handler is to hold on and stay out of the dog's way.

My days consisted of hours of classroom study learning about the role police dogs play, their proper application and laws, and case law police officers have to follow to use them properly. There were weekly fill-in-the-blank tests on the information. These were brutal. Each day had intervals of obedience work, and slowly I was introduced to the more complicated tasks of odor work, tracking, and apprehension.

The school was about an hour and a half from my home. I would get there at 7 a.m. and work until 4 p.m. Monday through Friday. They were long, stressful, but most of all rewarding days. I had twelve weeks to learn to trust Niko so I could be successful at my job. I had great instructors who were patient with me and knowledgeable about all the disciplines my job entailed. Gradually, I got better at relying on Niko. I believe that had I been paired with a new dog, I would not have succeeded in this course. I would have passed the tests but would have failed miserably at everything else. Niko carried our team.

Niko would continue to teach me lessons during our short partnership. There were times when I got it right and definitely times when I got it wrong. The times that stick out the most are when I had no idea what he was trying to tell me, but he still got it right.

My philosophy in being effective was a statistical approach. The more traffic stops I made, the more chances I would get to use my dog in his primary function: narcotics detection. I wanted to use him a lot, so I stopped a lot of cars. Now my approach to issuing tickets is this: You're only getting a ticket if

- **you really deserve it.** An example of this might be blatantly running a red light and almost striking a pedestrian while you're on the phone eating a sandwich (true story).

- **you talk yourself into it.** Officers are taught that the goal of traffic enforcement is voluntary compliance. So if I walk up to the car and tell you, "You were speeding," and you reply, "I'm sorry, it won't happen again," I have reason to believe you might comply in the future. You get a warning. If your reply is "No, I wasn't," then since no responsibility is taken, you probably won't voluntarily comply in the future, so . . . ticket. I have proudly led my department in warnings for years!

- **the dog tells me to.** If he tells me there is more to the traffic stop than a brake light that's out or going fifteen miles per hour over the speed limit, you are probably getting a ticket.

I vividly remember working the night shift (6 p.m. to 6 a.m.) one evening and pulling over a dark-colored coupe. I walked up to the window of the vehicle, introduced myself, and told the driver the reason for the stop. If I remember correctly, a brake light was out. I explained it to the driver as I had hundreds of times to other drivers. Usually the conversation goes like this:

Me: Hey [I always try to keep things informal and friendly], I'm Officer Tappan. The reason for the stop is you have a brake light out.

Them: [They typically look in the direction of the brake lights.] Really? Which one?

Me: The _____ [insert your favorite brake
   light]. Would you like to see? [Only if they have
   a passenger who can step on the brake so
   they can see it.]
Them: Wow, I'll get that fixed.
Me: Okay, have a great night!

This conversation was different. The driver's hands were clenched around the steering wheel to the point that his knuckles were white. His head was locked forward, his eyes staring into empty space. I could see his carotid artery pulsating rapidly. All of these signs indicated he was either nervous about something other than the brake light or he was having a medical episode. So I asked, "Is everything okay? It seems your heart is beating kind of fast. Is there something in the car that shouldn't be?"

Fun fact: most people are not good liars. I believe that we are all image bearers of God and he has written his law on our hearts. We know what's right, we just don't always do it! Which is why I got the following answer from the driver: "There shouldn't be." Think about it: He wasn't saying "No, there isn't." The claim was really that he either didn't know or he was agreeing with my question, that yes, there was something in the car but it shouldn't be there according to the law. Either way, it was Niko time.

The rule for using a dog on a traffic stop for narcotics detection is that you can use it on any traffic stop as long as it doesn't prolong the stop beyond the normal time it would take to perform all the checks and write a citation. You can extend it beyond that time if you can explain that you have a reasonable suspicion that another crime is being committed. Because of the driver's nervous behavior and the answer he gave, I fell into the second slot: believing he had something in the car that was illegal.

The great thing about the shift I was on is that all the officers loved working together. The minute one of us would pull out on a traffic stop, at least one other officer would head in the same direction to help if they could. Traffic stops can turn into dangerous situations very fast, so it is always good to have backup officers. Plus, the guys on my shift loved to see Niko work.

I had the driver get out of the vehicle and told him I was going to have my police dog do a sniff of the exterior. I gave the driver one more chance to be honest with me and tell me whether there was anything in the car. He said there was nothing he knew of. I had him stand with my backup and went to my police SUV to fetch my more highly qualified partner.

I began as I always did when I started as a handler—at the front of the vehicle—and gave Niko the command to sniff for narcotics: "*Such*" (German for track, pronounced "tsuk"). With me holding his leash, he began at the front license plate, then sniffed at nose level around the car to the driver's side. As he sniffed the bottom seam of the back part of the driver's door, his head snapped back toward the front area of the car. He pulled me along the seam of the driver's door, his sniffing increasing. This told me that Niko detected the odor of narcotics. He was trained as an active-alert dog, which meant his next indicator was to begin scratching at the location the odor was coming from. This coupe had seen better years, but Niko added some character to the driver's door with his paws. I did what I typically do in these situations. I stopped watching Niko on his active alert, locked eyes with the driver—who could see Niko scratching away at his beloved car door—and feigned a look of surprise (it was almost never true surprise). Then Niko ceased scratching, backed up a step, and put his furry butt on the ground.

Thanks to the confidence the courts have put in properly trained detection dogs, the encounter had now changed from suspicion of a crime to something called probable cause. This meant I could now search the car. I scratched Niko on the head and exclaimed in what we call a praise voice, "Aww, dat's a good boi!" (Dogs understand tone more than the meaning of a word, so part of K9 school is mastering a high-pitched praise voice that lets the dog know you are happy.) He got lots of praise as we walked back to his kennel in my police car.

I put on latex gloves at my car, then began the search of the vehicle. Every part of the car except the driver's seat was littered with trash, old mail, and clothing, so you couldn't see the seats or floorboard. I began where Niko alerted, on the driver's side, but I couldn't find anything because of all the filth. I switched to the other side because sometimes odor can behave in a way that you don't expect. I couldn't find anything there either. I was getting frustrated because I couldn't locate what Niko so easily smelled from outside the vehicle. If only I had something that could pinpoint the location! Oh wait, I did.

I retrieved Niko from his kennel to help me again. His tail was wagging excessively because of all the fun we'd just had. He could not wait to play the find-the-smell game again. This time he could play *inside* the vehicle! I walked him up to the open driver's door and gave him the track command, "Such!" Niko sniffed again, poked his head into the car right behind the driver's door, nose down into the pile of filth, and quickly sat and looked at me as if to say, "Hey, I already told you it was right here!" While holding the leash, I peeked in and moved some things around but still didn't see anything. I looked at Niko, doubt entering my mind. *Did he mess up? Did he false alert?* "Show me," I said. This was not even a command for Niko, but he understood. I needed more guidance. He buried his head into the pile of trash and from it pulled an envelope. He dropped it on the ground. I was confused. It was a regular-sized partially sealed envelope that appeared to be a bill, with the clear panels on the front. I had seen this envelope during the search but thought nothing of it because there were dozens more all throughout the car. I withheld praise from Niko because I wasn't sure whether he deserved it. He looked at me as if to say, "There it is, now give me love, and possibly my ball because I did awesome."

I opened the part of the envelope that was unsealed.

Inside was a small ziplock bag with a clear white crystalline substance. I field-tested it to make sure, but I knew right then it was crystal methamphetamine. Niko got scratches on the head, the high praise voice, and his highest reward: his toy for doing such an excellent job. The other officer looked on in disbelief and exclaimed, "Did he just pull that out of the car for you?!" He sure did! Both of us were amazed at Niko's precision. I was learning to listen to my partner. Together we could be a great team.

Taking Care of Each Other

Being a good team means both of us contribute and complement each other. I downplay the role the handler has, but ours really is an important one. You have to drive around, type all the reports, groom, feed, provide good training, interpret the dog's messages, and protect it from situations that could cause it harm (among myriad other things).

About a year and a half into our partnership, I started noticing a cloudiness in Niko's left eye. I would throw a ball and could tell he was definitely having trouble tracking it on that side. I was concerned for him, but he was still highly functional at most of his work. At our department, it is the responsibility of the handler to care for the dogs and inform decision-makers when there may be a problem that needs to be addressed. I didn't fully grasp how it could affect our work. The danger it posed came to a head one evening.

A 911 call came in around 2:30 a.m. about a violent domestic dispute. A man had attacked his wife with a pipe and fled the scene. When you hear a call like that, it grabs the attention of every officer working. We had a great team on shift, so everyone knew exactly what to do. Two officers go to the scene to get good information about what happened. The second officer on scene directs others to where they may be most helpful by setting up a perimeter of the scene based on how long ago the suspect fled. Niko and I would respond to the last place the suspect was known to be and go after him. Typically, I would take another officer with me for safety. We got there so quickly that no one else had arrived yet, and we had major holes in the perimeter. Time was ticking and the longer we waited, the more likely it was that the guy would get away. I made the call: Niko and I were hitting the ground for a track.

I threw on Niko's tracking harness and grabbed my twenty-foot-long leash. As I was getting ready to begin the track, we got more information about the suspect from our dispatch. "He was a Special Forces operator, home on leave, and possibly suffering from PTSD." This raised the danger significantly. He was highly trained, especially for evasion and combat. The officer on scene with the victim confirmed that they had evidence of aggravated battery (unwanted physical contact with another that causes serious bodily harm: broken bones or other damage that is long lasting). I needed to wait for a backup officer. Just then someone keyed up that they were thirty seconds out. I gave my starting location—the apartment complex he'd fled from—and told the backup to catch up with us on the track.

I took Niko to the bottom of the stairwell of the apartment the suspect had run from and told Niko to lie down. This let him know we were about to start a track from that location. I think it's utterly fascinating what the dog processes in that moment. He must ascertain the one unique human odor that he smells there but is no longer present. That's the one he has to find. In situations like this, it is likely that the suspect is experiencing fear, anxiety, and probably an excess of adrenaline. This helps the dog track because it has something called a vomeronasal organ that detects pheromones your body releases. Niko was getting excited and started inching forward toward where he last smelled the suspect in anticipation of his command to track.

Niko loved this game. We did it often, usually about an hour a day every day we worked. I told Niko, "Such!" As he always did, he let out a tiny bark of excitement, his body rose while his nose stayed glued to the ground, and he walked at a moderate pace. He was methodical at this discipline, taking his time so as not to miss a single smell, determined and focused on the exact odor he was tracking. My backup officer fell into place adjacent and behind our track, keeping an eye out in the direction we were heading.

The three of us skirted the wood line behind the apartment complex leading to a road. Niko's head popped up, indicating he had lost the ground scent of the suspect because of the asphalt and the multiple cars that had disrupted the path of the track. He knew what to do; he just searched the air for the scattered odor on the other side of the street and then at the edge put his nose down and worked along the street until he found the ground odor again. His head snapped perpendicular to the road; boom, he was on it again. We were heading toward a park in the area.

Niko approached a concessions building in the park and pulled me toward the girls' bathroom on the left side of the building. He lay down by the door and sniffed the space between the bottom of the door and the concrete. I pushed open the door, and the automatic lights in the bathroom came on. Niko went to the left side of the bathroom, passing the first stall and slightly glancing in. Then he started to circle to his right as I was passing the first stall on my left.

I felt uneasy. Like I was being watched. Typically, the rule for tracking is to keep your eyes on your dog, but instinctively I glanced into the stall Niko had passed on the left. There I saw the suspect, crouched and clutching a bloody metal pipe. I drew my gun from my holster as Niko circled back to my side. Niko showed a flash of his teeth, sensing this was the object of our track. With that, the suspect dropped the pipe compliantly, and my backup took him into custody.

Relief and concern hit me simultaneously. Relief in a job well done but concern as to why Niko hadn't seen the guy. I was lucky neither Niko nor I got hurt. The what-ifs ran through my head over and over, terrifying me with the possible horrible outcomes that could have happened because he didn't lock onto the suspect. That's when I realized he couldn't see at all out of his left eye. It was clear it wasn't safe for him to work as a protection dog any longer. I had to make the hard decision of presenting to my department that Niko should be retired at only six years old.

When a K9 retires, the department allows the handler to adopt it. I was told I would get another K9 partner, which would make it difficult to keep Niko. He was not good with other working dogs, and I knew this would present a problem. I had to make the decision to give Niko to a friend of mine. This was a very difficult decision, and I'm pretty sure my oldest daughter is still mad at me for it. My friend was a single mom and dog trainer. She was going to use Niko as a stud dog and train more police dogs on a large open farm in North Carolina. I didn't care to explain to my kids how good a life this was for him, and I am sure you can see why!

About two years after Niko went to his happy retirement on the farm, my friend called to let me know Niko had a litter of puppies and asked me if I wanted to come see them. My wife and kids and I took a trip up to the farm. Even though I hadn't seen Niko in two years, the moment I turned into the driveway, he came running. I opened the car door and was attacked with his tongue. Soon there were happy tears coming down my face.

For the two hours we stayed there it was like he and I had never been apart. His puppies climbed all over my kids and me, nipping and barking. I reflected the entire time on the value of learning to listen to a dog. Saying good-bye to him that day was hard, but the phone call I got on August 16, 2020, was harder. Here is the text of the email I sent to my department:

> It is with great sadness I pass along my first K9 partner Niko has passed. He served the city from 2011–2015 before he retired for loss of vision in one of his eyes. He was a faithful partner, and I am forever grateful for his service and friendship.

I loved that dog so much. He taught me about how to trust my K9 partner and not just rely on my own instincts. He was such a good friend, and I couldn't have asked for a better teacher. He wasn't the perfect dog, and I was definitely not the perfect handler, but together we made a really good team. Niko helped me realize that if I was going to be any good as a handler—or in any relationship—my pride would need to be eliminated.

START WITH A SOLID FOUNDATION

"Everyone who hears these words of mine and puts them into practice is like a wise man who built his house on the rock."
—MATTHEW 7:24

Like I mentioned in lesson 2, my mom always told me I could do anything I wanted if I was willing to put in the work. That was my formula to win: outwork everyone else.

Taking Over Training

My second year in K9—when the initial feeling of drinking from a firehose and learning the new job had subsided—I started to realize something: our K9 unit was in a bit of a complacency rut. Training consisted of talking, running a drill or two to meet the minimum standard, our annual certification, and then calling it a day after a maximum of four hours. Rinse and repeat every two weeks. For someone like me, who was highly driven toward being the best I could, this was incredibly frustrating. We were doing the bare minimum. We weren't outworking anyone.

It all came to a head for me after one particular training session. Even though it was a holiday, we still had training scheduled. This didn't bother me at all. I had made arrangements with my family and gone in ready to work. But less than an hour after we started training, the decision was made to call it a day.

I approached the K9 commander and told him how disappointed I was with the level at which we were training and that we could do better. His response was impressive. He accepted responsibility and challenged me. "Then you do it. Find a trainer's course and you take over training." I'm not sure if this was out of frustration at my assessment or great leadership and taking responsibility. I didn't care because I saw it as an opportunity to go to another level in our training. He told me to find a trainer's school to get my certification as a police K9 trainer.

After that conversation, I was invigorated. I scoured the internet to find a school and saw an upcoming K9 training conference featuring many K9 schools that offered a trainer's certification. The whole K9 unit registered and attended. One course immediately stood out among all the others. It wasn't because of anything the lead trainer and owner said but the way that his sixty-five-pound Malinois followed him around—off leash—through masses of people and a few barking dogs. The Malinois, Abby, had complete focus on Jeff, the lead trainer, and waited for any command, verbal or nonverbal, to fervently respond to him. Jeff and Abby did a demonstration by their booth in the middle of the jam-packed vendor hall, showing Abby's prowess in the discipline of apprehension. With a wave of Jeff's hand and a whispered word, Abby took off at a full sprint (if you have never seen a Malinois in full sprint, it is absolutely fluid and poetic, but if you blink, you will miss it) and launched herself effortlessly into the air, jaw open and teeth prepped to clamp down on the arm of a decoy wearing a protective suit. With the momentum Abby had accumulated, the decoy spun around and *wham*, slammed to the ground. With another word from Jeff, Abby instantly released the decoy and pranced back to his left side with her tail wagging happily. She looked up into Jeff's eyes, waiting for the next task. They were completely in sync!

No other dog at the conference had this level of control. The "out" (when a dog releases the decoy) is usually a frustrating battle of wills between what the dog wants (to continue biting) and what the handler wants (to stop biting). In police certification it is the part you fear the most: whether your dog will "out" when it is supposed to. Abby did it with apparent joy. She was also able to go anywhere with Jeff and interact with people, and he would let them pet her with absolutely no fear that she would snap and bite. Actually, if she wasn't on a task Jeff had put her to, she would approach you and lean all of her sixty-five pounds into your leg to try to get some scratches on the back.

In that one demonstration I saw a level of control I had never seen in any police dog. The ones I had seen were always on edge. There is a reason they wore the Do Not Pet patches. To see Abby calm, focused, and efficient was such a special thing, and it made it clear to me that Jeff and Abby had a unique bond.

I spent the next two days of the conference speaking to the other training schools. Some were impressive, but Jeff didn't just talk a good game—he had proof in Abby that no one else did. I asked him how he and Abby were so connected, and he said it was first about choosing the right dog and then the amount of quality work you put into the dog. This advice resonated with me: start on a good foundation and outwork what others do. I signed up for his next trainer's course scheduled for December 2014.

Cobra Canine

I drove the four hours up to Cobra Canine, located in a small town outside Nashville, Tennessee. It was a twelve-week course, with the first four weeks consisting of Jeff and me training dogs for an upcoming handler's course and the final eight weeks constituting that course. There is a lesson to be learned just in the math: it takes twice as long to teach the people as it does to teach the dogs.

I was the only one in the trainer's course, so I was Jeff's shadow. The course was slotted for eight-hour days, but I was away from my family and my only purpose for being there was to learn. So I stayed from the moment the doors were open until Jeff finished his last class (he taught basic obedience in the evening to civilian customers). I loved every second and learned so much. Jeff was an incredible trainer with a work ethic not many could match.

Jeff's first lesson for me was in how to select a good police dog. He had myriad tests he would put dogs through to determine whether they had the right focus and effort to be a good police dog. He explained that the three most important characteristics were that the dog be happy, social, and confident.

I found it odd that Jeff started with a happy dog. As I said before, that is not how I would describe most police dogs. Neurotic, on edge, or angry were more appropriate descriptions in my experience. But he explained you can never trust a dog that doesn't have a happy disposition. A dog that is on edge or angry may decide to act without command. Typically, to train dogs like that, you must use more compulsive-type training, which creates conflict. He said a happy dog wants to make you happy. Those were the words I had heard my dad say for years: "Son, all that dog wants is to make you happy."

Sociability in dogs means they adapt to any situation, condition, or experience you put them in. Some dogs have issues in noisy atmospheres, don't like certain surfaces, or are spooked by random things. In police work you must be able to trust that your dog can be effective in any circumstance or place.

Confidence is the belief the dog has that he can be successful. If a dog doesn't believe he can do something, he may not even try, or he might back out of a situation once it doesn't go as planned.

We put these criteria to work in selecting dozens of dogs for upcoming classes and to fulfill government contracts Jeff had to provide trained dogs to Special Forces units. Through repetition of the selection process and then training the dogs selected, I started to pick up on what would make a good police dog.

The next part of the equation was making me a good trainer. There is so much frustration when you're first learning to train dogs because it's like trying to communicate in a language you don't yet speak. I am not a great verbal processor; I learn better by experiential methods. When I used to compete in karate tournaments, my coach would tell me to keep my hands up. While I understood the words he spoke and would nod to communicate that I received the message, my hands wouldn't move. My coach would then punch me in the face and instantly my hands would go up to protect my face. I needed the punch in the face to fully grasp the lesson.

So it is in dog training. One day in front of a class out in a field, I was getting frustrated with a dog because sometimes he would kneel and sometimes he wouldn't. Jeff yelled across the field that I was the one screwing up, not the dog. Punch in the face. I was doing something different each time with the dog. I wasn't being consistent, so neither was the dog. It was embarrassing because I was supposed to be teaching the students, but Jeff had told me the same thing in private and I hadn't responded. I wasn't mad, I just finally understood. I had to be consistent. (By the way, if you want to be a great dog trainer, be consistent.)

Canine Testing

Niko retired right after I finished the school in the spring of 2015, and it was time for me to select my next dog. I knew what I wanted thanks to my time with Jeff—a dog just like Abby. We call them pocket rocket Malinois. One thing I learned with Niko is that large German shepherds take a toll on your body, especially when you are on the smaller side. So I thought a sixty-pound Belgian Malinois as my next partner would be perfect.

In August 2015 I found a school in Fort McClellan, Alabama, not too far from home. The school had a good selection of what I was looking for. I scheduled a day before the training course to test their dogs. They had a trailer full of dogs they thought would fit what I was looking for, as well as one dog that was training for another discipline that they wanted to get some exercise. They explained that that dog was supposed to be a personal protection dog but the buyer had backed out.

The first three tests I conducted were to assess prey drive, hunt drive, and perseverance.

Test #1: Prey Drive

For prey drive the test is simple. You take the dog's toy and throw it as far as you can. You are looking to see how intensely it runs after the toy. This test displays the value the dog places on the toy and how much it likes the game of chasing prey. It translates to police work in a few ways. The obvious is chasing a suspect, but it also shows whether the dog will respond to toy-driven training methods in which you use the toy as a reward.

I started running the nine dogs the school was showing

me through the drills and was impressed with some but not so much with others. I had a scoring system of 1–5: 1 would be a dog with little to no interest, while 5 meant you believed that the toy was the most important thing in the world to it. Most of the dogs were landing in the 3 or 4 range. There was one Mal that looked very similar to Abby named Major, and he got a solid 4. I think I bumped him up to a 4.2 just because of his looks.

Finally, one of the kennel techs went and got the last dog, the one they wanted to test. It leapt out of the dog trailer. It was a humungous bicolor German shepherd. He was beautiful, almost solid black with golden paws. My very first thoughts when I saw the dog were *He's too big and he's a German shepherd. I definitely don't want that one.* Every other dog would enthusiastically drag the kennel techs to the testing area, pulling and lunging because they knew they were going to do something they loved. This dog walked calmly. I was certain he would be less than motivated to chase a ball. As the kennel tech passed the leash off to me, he smirked and said, "We call him the Cadillac." No other explanation.

I cocked my arm to throw the ball, and instantly the calm vanished into a focused determination. The Cadillac lowered his frame like an Olympic sprinter waiting for the gun to sound, every muscle fiber maximized to reach his goal. I threw the ball and he was off, fast like his life depended on it but graceful and in control. Nothing else mattered in the world but that ball. I scribbled down on my paper: "5! But too big."

Test #2: Hunt Drive

Next up was to test the dogs' hunt drive: how hard they will look for something that they can smell but not see. For this test you throw the ball while holding on to the dog until the ball hits the ground. Spin the dog around a couple of times so it loses its visual cues and bearing and then let it go hunt for the ball. It translates to police work in that you need a dog to rely on its sense of smell to find a reward, and to track someone it must find satisfaction in the hunt itself. This test weeds out a lot of dogs because many will lose interest or be distracted during the search. It's not about how fast they find the object but more about how hard they look.

Honestly, this had been a weakness of Niko's. He would get distracted by other animal odors on a track. He liked to hunt, but there were other things he liked more. It was always a point of frustration, so this test was important to me. Scores for the dogs ranged from 2 to 3. Squirrels would run across the trail and their heads would pop up. One dog peed on a stump while looking for the ball, and every dog after him got distracted by the pee. Some would mark over it, then continue the hunt. Major did well—he got a 3, the best of the bunch . . . until the Cadillac. The second the Cadillac was let loose, the hunt was all that mattered. The pee and the squirrels did not exist to him, only the hunt for his prize. I believe the ground could have been littered with juicy T-bones and Cadillac would have cruised right over them. My notes said, "5, but he's a German shepherd."

Test #3: Perseverance

The last of the ball tests was perseverance. The way we do this is to tease the dog with the ball and place it in a location the dog can see and smell but can't get to. In our case we had a fifty-pound wooden pallet we placed the ball under. This is important to police work because you want to see if the dog, when presented with an obstacle to the goal, will still try hard to get to it.

Scores were back to 3 to 4 on this one. Dogs would dig and try to fit their heads through the slats in the pallet but to no avail. A couple tried to get under it, but I was standing on the pallet so they couldn't. Most would start to bark at it in frustration. This was usually the sign they had exhausted their options. Major again was a solid 4. For the Cadillac the test was over almost before it began. He immediately saw the ball and the obstacle. He grabbed the pallet with his teeth and flipped it—and consequently me as well—snatching the ball and trotting around with his prize in his mouth. I didn't get to test his perseverance because he got to it so quickly, but he demonstrated something that is very hard to test: problem-solving. I wrote down "6 . . . Maybe." I was falling in love with this dog.

———

After these tests we took a break for lunch, and I started asking questions about the Cadillac. They said he wasn't ready for a police course because he hadn't been trained in odor detection or tracking. His name was Cayman. I liked the name, but it was too close to my son's name, Cayden. Another reason not to get him. Every one of the kennel techs loved him because he was levelheaded and did everything smooth, like riding in a Cadillac. They explained that some of the dogs have you wondering whether they might kill you, but with Cayman the Cadillac you could tell he was just happy to be working.

This put a check in the box of the most important characteristic: happy.

Bite Tests

After testing for prey drive, hunt drive, and perseverance, next up were the bite tests. I was looking forward to them because—and I may sound a little crazy here—it gave me a really good idea of how intense a dog is. I donned the padded suit we call a bite suit and got ready for a gamut of different bite scenarios. The bite suit I liked to wear was as thin as they make them, and it usually kept the dog's teeth from penetrating, but I could still feel a lot of pressure and would definitely bruise from a hard-biting dog.

Passive Bite Test

The first test was a passive bite test. It is an advanced assessment that checks the level a dog is at. When dogs start performing bite work, they need a lot of stimulation to agitate them: yelling, snapping of whips (I should say here the whips are used only for the audial cue, never used on the dog), or clatter sticks. Advanced dogs bite because they are aimed at a target and told, "I need you to go bite that." You must have a dog that will bite simply because you tell it to. In law enforcement work your life may depend on it, and the perpetrator may not be screaming, flailing, or doing any of the usual things that upset a dog to the point of biting.

All you do for this test is stand in a corner, facing away from the dog, with your arms tucked up by your chest (so the dog doesn't target your unprotected hands). Then the handler sends the dog on a bite command. Most of the dogs did okay. You could tell they were used to agitation because they would reluctantly bite.

The next part of the passive bite test is to see if they stay on the bite even if you don't fight back. The dogs love the guy in the fluffy suit because most of the time it means a super fun game of tug with a really authentic sounding squeaky toy. That's not a test. If you give no sound, no tug, no eye contact, no reaction at all, will the dog continue to do what you ask? Some of the dogs stayed on, some popped off the bite and re-bit, and some just walked around confused.

When dogs know they are going to do bite work, they get fired up. You could hear the dogs communicating with each other in the trailer outside our training area. They would bark, "Hey, other dogs, we are doing bite work!" The other dogs would respond incessantly with barks of excitement so that by the time they entered the room they had worked themselves into a barely controllable fluffy ball of enthusiastic rage. They would enter like UFC fighters at the weigh-in face-off. They'd lock eyes with the guy in the fluffy suit and pull.

When Cayman strolled into the room, the difference between him and the rest of the dogs was immediately clear. He was calm and focused. I was sitting on the arm of a couch not far from the door, and I saw him do something in that moment that struck me as incredible. You could tell he heard the dog commotion and knew exactly what was about to go down. Rather than lock on me in the bite suit, his head whipped back and forth, eyeing every warm body in that room. He didn't care whether they were in protective suits or not.

Most apprehension dogs develop something called equipment fixation from training with bite suits, sleeves, and agitating sounds. So much so that when they are sent on a "real" bite, they don't know what to do. It can be catastrophic if it happens, and I have seen it happen multiple times. You must train intentionally with muzzles and hidden equipment to ensure this doesn't happen. It was clear Cayman had zero equipment fixation.

I calmly walked over to the corner, tucked my arms, and gave a nod the handler could notice. I heard the Dutch command for bite: "*Stellen!*" I heard toenails on the tile floor rapidly approaching. I felt the thud of one hundred pounds of energy in motion being transferred into my body. Then I felt the most intense, crushing pressure I have ever felt just above the elbow of my right arm. I tried not to react, but it was difficult. He didn't care if I made a sound, pulled, made eye contact, or did anything. Somehow, throughout the passive bite, he crushed increasingly harder until I painfully grunted "Okay" to signal to the handler he could call him off the bite. I tried to write down a 10 on the 1–5 scale, but I couldn't hold the pen in my right hand.

Pressure on the Bite

Next test was to determine how the dog responds to pressure. In my experience, suspects respond to a K9's attack in one of three ways: they remain passive; they scream and react in pain but try to comply to make the pain stop; or they fight. This test measures how well the dog reacts when you fight and put the dog in uncomfortable situations. It is like a sparring session where both parties are giving and taking. It's all about timing and feel. And it is paramount that the decoy in the suit is experienced and knows how to apply pressure at the right time without hurting the dog.

I had three things set up. The first was a wooden desk the dog would have to leap onto, where he would engage the bite while elevated on a slippery surface. Then while the dog was on the desk, I would pull him off and hold him on my shoulder while he was still engaged, and finally I would lead him onto a light metal folding chair that would fall over and clang on the tile floor, making a loud noise. In that one test you get to see sociability, confidence, and perseverance.

Once again, the dogs did as I expected. Some popped off for a brief second but then reengaged. I scored them as 3s across the board.

In came Cayman the Cadillac. I was standing behind the desk right at the edge so I could keep his paws on the surface of the desk. "Stellen!" I saw him coming this time . . . I think. It all happened so fast. Intensity, focus, intelligence, power, and energy exploded over the desk, clamping onto my right armpit and flinging me backward off my feet and partway through the wood-paneled wall behind me, knocking over the chair in the process. From my back I anemically uttered, "He's good." One of the trainers rushed over and said, "No, do your other little tests." With a smile on his face, as if he knew something I didn't, he helped me to my feet, with Cayman still crushing my shoulder, and set up the folding chair.

I lifted Cayman onto the desk. He bit harder. I swung him into the chair. He bit harder. He wasn't like a Cadillac; he was like a race car that always finds another gear to go harder. While he continued crushing my shoulder from the front, I tried to step over him with my left leg, putting him between my legs in a very uncomfortable situation. Apparently he knew this move since he pulled backward as I stepped, effectively pulling my right arm through my legs and flipping me onto my back, with him on top of me. This was the greatest dog I had ever seen.

The trainer who knew something came over, still smiling, scratched Cayman's head, patted me on the chest, and told Cayman to release, which he did promptly. I found out later that the trainer was a guy named Cody Tallent. In my opinion, he's one of the best decoys in the world. He clearly had a passion for dogs, and he stands out in the K9 world. He had poured a lot of time and energy into Cayman, and he told me that Cayman was one of the best dogs he had ever worked with. Over the course of the time I spent in Alabama, we became good friends and I learned so much from him.

Cayman had checked all the boxes: happy, social, and confident. I told the school I wanted him. They reminded me that he wasn't ready for a police course because he didn't know tracking or detection. I explained that I didn't care, I would teach him. They agreed, and the greatest dog I had ever seen was about to become my partner!

A Name to Live Up To

One thing remained, though: he needed a new name. I could not be confusing Cayman every time I said my son's name or vice versa. It wouldn't do to have my nine-year-old thinking I was yelling at him to get in his kennel and go to sleep.

He needed a name that captured his strength, intelligence, and calm intensity. A name to be lived up to. Something that conveyed both *mighty warrior* and *strategic thinker*. Since I am a former marine, it didn't take long for me to make the connection to the most legendary modern-day general in the Marine Corps. They called him the "Warrior Monk." He has more motivational quotes to his name than any other general. He was respected by everyone who served under him and feared by any enemy who faced him. Chuck Norris wears underwear with his likeness on it. His name: General James "Mad Dog" Mattis.

Out of the bite suit, I leaned down and scratched the Cadillac's head. "Mattis, you think you can live up to that, buddy?" He laid his head on my shoulder as if to say, "I will, and I like you too!"

Mattis had all the God-given traits he would need to be an excellent police dog. He was as perfect a foundation to start with as I could imagine. Now it was up to me to not screw him up!

PERSISTENCE PAYS OFF

Blessed is the man who remains steadfast.

—JAMES 1:12 ESV

It was Alabama in August 2015, and the weather was exactly what you would expect: thick, sticky, and hot! I chose the Fort McClellan school because of the setting (and the amazing dog I'd found). The school had an expansive and diverse environment in which to train a dog: abandoned barracks, parking lots, roads, and shops that were perfect for urban training. But also open fields, streams, hills, and densely wooded areas. I remember thinking, as I had many times in my life before starting something new and unknown, *All right, here we go. Bring it!* The difference this time was that I wouldn't be facing it by myself; I had Mattis with me.

Another reason I selected this school was because they trained their dogs to a higher standard than most. In addition to a certification from the school, if you were successful, you would get a highly respected national certification. This would not be an easy task.

I was already sweating through my shirt as the other students and I gathered early in the morning of the first day. I was giddy with excitement because I couldn't wait to start working with Mattis. That would have to wait, though; first days were filled with administration and logistics. We met the instructors, toured the grounds, signed waivers, and then, finally, we got to swing by the kennels.

This would be the first time I got to see Mattis since I had selected him.

Yips and barks from dozens of dogs echoed throughout the kennel as we walked in. When dogs are in an environment like that, some will spin in circles, the Malinois will tend to jump and test the confines of their kennels, and almost all of them will be barking. As I was walking through, I noticed that each dog had a plexiglass placard hanging on the outside of the kennel with its name written in temporary marker. I saw that the placard of the upcoming kennel had the clean outline of the name Cayman, which had been erased, and the name Mattis written over it. Then I saw him. He wasn't spinning, leaping, or barking. He was standing at the front of his kennel, as if he were the overseer. He saw me and his demeanor changed. He went from standing stoically to his mouth dropping open slightly and his tongue popping out the side, and he leaned up against the front of the kennel to get a scratch from me.

All the feelings I had when I selected him were reinforced in that moment. I knelt and whispered, "We are going to crush this!" I knew we were starting behind all the other teams because he needed to learn nose work, but he exuded intelligence, and I was confident in his abilities. I had no doubts the words I whispered would be truth. Little did I know, an extra twist was about to be thrown our way, a setback that would complicate everything.

Training with Mattis

The first exercise we would do with our dogs was a familiarization walk. Nothing fancy, just taking your new police partner for a walk with twelve other police dogs in close proximity. On this walk I was reminded why he was nicknamed the Cadillac. The eleven other dogs were darting back and forth at the end of their six-foot leashes, dragging their partners all over the place in a combination of curiosity at the smells of the world and fury directed toward the other dogs.

Apparently Mattis had read the curriculum ahead of time and understood that that behavior was not the intention of this walk. He knew it was for us to get acquainted, so he looked up at me, awaiting instruction, and I gave it to him. While walking, I shortened the leash and moved my left shoulder back. He put his shoulder on my knee, looked up at my face, and pranced like a show horse among the chaos. It was the best "heel" I had ever seen a police dog do.

I knew his commands were in Dutch, but I wasn't super familiar with them all yet, so I just relied on hand motions to start. With my right hand in front of my body, I lifted my palm upward, from my beltline to my chest. Midstride, Mattis stopped and sat as I let the leash slip from my hand and continued to walk. Lunging, barking, and pulling were going on all around us, but there sat Mattis, like a statue, his gaze locked on me waiting for his next command. I stopped walking away, faced Mattis, then motioned with my hand, palm down, from my chest to my waist. His front paws shot out from under him, and he lay down in place. His motion was intentional and fast, sparing no extra movements.

This obedience command, a down stay, was important because one of the most difficult tasks for a high-drive dog is to do nothing. You ask the dog to lie down, away from you, and do nothing for a couple of minutes. Every certification has this command in its tests, and it is one of the most nerve-racking. The dog hates it, the handler hates it, and the evaluator loves it. You can usually see the dog getting antsy, looking around, licking his lips, yawning, then getting up and walking to the handler. The handler usually responds by yelling words in Dutch or Czech or German, trying to get the dog to stay.

Mattis saw the command and understood that he was supposed to stay down until he was asked to do something else. I could have left, had lunch, and come back. He would have been in the same spot waiting for a command. He was content. There was no confusion or frustration. He understood the assignment. Three minutes later, I held my left hand out to my side at a thirty-degree angle, palm facing Mattis, and moved my left shoulder back. He came sprinting to my left side, spun around so he was facing the same direction I was, put his shoulder on my knee, and looked up at me in a perfect sitting heel. I gave him his toy, which was a rubber toy with a rope through it, and we played tug.

The whole hour we were out there we had a blast. He was amazing.

Other handlers would try some obedience here and there, but it would turn into a battle of wills, and that was not really what the walk was about. It was about building trust. The other dogs were reluctant with their trust, but Mattis, for some reason, already trusted me. This gesture was not lost on me. It may sound odd, but I felt honored that he would give me his trust, and I wanted him to know I trusted him as well. Man, this dog was good!

━━━

I knew every other dog at the school was trained the same way, but for whatever reason, Mattis was different, special, and very intuitive. I would stay late every day and teach him odor work, most of the time with the help of Cody. Detection is one of my favorite skills to teach a dog. There are many crazy theories on how you teach a dog to find an odor (I've heard some say you get the dog addicted to drugs!), but it really is a simple game that taps into his prey drive and perseverance. You show the dog a ball, tease him, and while he can still see you, you drop it into a box with a hole on the top. The box contains the odor you are trying to teach the dog. The dog runs to the box, and as he puts his head close to it, the ball pops up from a spring-loaded contraption. If the dog catches the ball in the air, everything is fine in the world for him; if not, chaos ensues until he chases down the only thing that matters in life to him—that ball! It is also important that you explode with joy—as if your child just won a gold medal in the Olympics—the moment the dog does what he is supposed to do. The more fun you make it, the more the dog wants to play the game.

You repeat this process over and over again. It is a super fun game for the dog, so much fun that he makes note in his brain of everything that he sees, smells, and does in the moment to make the ball spring into the air. After a few repetitions you add in a sit command right before the ball pops. Eventually the dog understands the game and will run up to the box, sniff it, and sit on his own. You start adding in other boxes with no odor to teach the dog it is only the box with the special odor that gets him rewarded.

Mattis understood the game quickly and thoroughly enjoyed it. We had a lot of fun. Ball pops, Mattis chases hard after it, and Cody and I squeal with joy at the amazing accomplishment every time! In the first week Mattis surpassed his fellow four-legged students in the class.

Tracking was the other element Mattis was behind on, but it is simple to teach. I would come in early to work with him on this, again usually with the help of Cody. It works like this: Have your helper tease your dog with a toy and run away to a place the dog can't see. Start the dog on an item the helper dropped, like a sweaty hat, then have the dog find him. As you progress, you want the dog to start using his nose, not his eyes, to identify the person who has his toy. So you remove the part where the dog sees the helper run away and just start him on the sweaty hat that was dropped. You make the tracks longer and longer with different types of ground and obstacles, and eventually you have an amazing tracking dog. The key to this one is, again, to flip out with excitement when the dog finds the helper and make it the most amazing time in the world.

On Friday of the first week, another student laid down a track for us. This would be the longest and most difficult one we had done to date. Mattis was progressing well, so I wanted to test his limits a bit. I waited about ten minutes after the student left and found the odor item that had been dropped. I told Mattis to lie down at the item. He began to sniff the item on his own. He was getting it! I told him to track, and we were off. I learned very quickly that Mattis had an extremely fast pace when tracking. Some dogs you need to slow down so they don't miss anything. Mattis was the opposite of that—he tracked better fast, so you better keep up (and be in good shape)!

The track started in a wooded area, and then we went through a field where I could actually see where the student had gone because the grass was smooshed down. Mattis was right on it. He led us to a road where he skirted alongside the edge. Then we came to a bridge that went over a stream about ten feet below. As we stepped onto the bridge, Mattis's head popped up from sniffing the ground to the railing of the bridge.

Without warning, he jumped off the bridge, following the odor. Luckily, I had a good grip on his leash, and I lowered him to the side of the stream below. This dog had no fear! I got down to where he was, and Mattis continued under the bridge to a water drainpipe on the other side. There sat the student. Mattis tracked like he had been doing it all his life. I had never seen a dog so fearless.

Mattis was ahead of the rest of the class. I was very proud of his progress and knew that the remaining five weeks of the abbreviated class gave me plenty of time to get him to the point where he would not only meet the standard he needed for certification but absolutely destroy it. On top of that, I couldn't wait to get this dog back to Alpharetta and start working with him. He was so good.

A Training Setback

On Monday morning of the second week, we started with a building search, something Mattis had never tried before. This is how it's done: You have a person in a bite suit hide inside a building, and the dog uses its nose to locate the decoy. Mattis picked it up easily and dragged me on a long leash through the building to a closed door. He could smell the odor of the bite suit and probably some fear emanating from under the seam of the door because the decoy knew it was Mattis—and that he bites hard. I held Mattis at the door, and the decoy popped the door open ever so slightly and yelled at Mattis (to build anticipation, making the game more fun) and then shut the door quickly. Mattis grabbed the bottom of the door with his teeth and ripped it in half. The instructors chuckled because they had never seen a dog do that before. They told me to let Mattis have him (telling me he could go bite the decoy). I dropped the leash and Mattis crawled through the opening he had created and engaged the decoy.

I went to grab Mattis off the bite and noticed he was licking his lips excessively, almost like he had just eaten some peanut butter. His top teeth looked good, bottom right looked good, but the bottom left tooth was cracked, and two-thirds of the visible tooth was gone.

This was really bad. For a personal pet it's no big deal, but for a dog in the middle of a training course it potentially spelled the end of his chance to be a police dog. He couldn't train until it was fixed because his motivation for training is either a toy to chew on or a person in a bite suit. Mattis couldn't do either because it would further damage the tooth and cause him pain, which would then give him a negative association with the work. With my hand on his shoulders, I sank to the floor, feeling sick to my stomach. He didn't know how this could affect him, but I did.

I brought it to the attention of the instructors, and soon I was sitting in an office with the owner of the company. He presented me with two options:

1. Pick out another dog and finish the program.
2. Get Mattis's tooth fixed with titanium and try to finish the program.

The difficulty with the second option was that it would take some time to get him fitted for the tooth. A mold had to be created and then put in. After that, I would have to wait on the glue to set for a couple of days. I was in week two of an abbreviated six-week course and all of that dental work would take at least four weeks. Four weeks of not being able to be rewarded with a toy.

The owner was clear: Mattis could not train with the class for those four weeks, and if he didn't pass the certification, we would have to be recycled to another class (which I knew my department would not allow). That would abruptly end my time in the K9 unit.

The smarter option was to pick another dog. The school had some really good options, and any of them would be able to pass the course. Or I could go with Mattis, and it might cost me being able to handle a dog ever again. If he didn't pass the course, it was likely he would be sold as a washout to someone else and I would never see him again. I had to ask myself, *Do I give up on the dog but keep my dream alive of being a handler, or risk it all for this dog that has already offered his trust to me?*

I said, "Let's get his tooth fixed; that dog is special!" I didn't go with the smart option. I'm a former marine and I go with what's right. That dog gave me his trust and broke his tooth ripping off a door to do a job I asked him to do. I refused to give up on him. In that moment I wasn't worried; I had complete confidence that we would find a way to make it work.

Looking back, it is easy to see the gravity of that decision. In the moment it was just the right thing to do. When you believe something, you hold fast, you stand firm, and you don't compromise. I believed this dog could be the best, and I knew I had a special connection with him. He wasn't the breed I initially wanted and he wasn't the size I had wanted, but he was meant to be my partner and I knew it. I knew that day that I was Team Mattis and that that wouldn't change.

I took him to the veterinarian dental specialist, and they rounded his remaining tooth and took measurements for the titanium implant. If that changed at all, I was in trouble. No ball, no hard rubber, no jute (tough woven materials used for bite toys). I had heard exactly what the owner had told me: "You can't train that dog *with the class*." He didn't say anything about early mornings or late nights in my hotel room. Yet I couldn't reward him with a toy. Training a dog is not hard when you figure out what they love. Mattis loved to bite things, so this was definitely a problem. I needed something we could play tug with that he would enjoy but would not damage his tooth at all.

I looked around my hotel room and spotted a face towel. I grabbed the towel, rolled it up, and presented it to Mattis. He understood. He grabbed ahold with his back teeth and wiggled his head around as I held on to the edges sticking out either side of his mouth. It was fun for him, and we had our solution to start training when no one was looking.

During classes I would help train the other dogs and

handlers. After class I would hang around the property, hide the towel in the woods, and have Mattis search for it. I had access to pseudo narcotics used for training purposes. These pseudo narcotics are scientifically formulated to replicate the odor of substances he is trained to find (methamphetamines, cocaine, and heroin). I would hide them and reward him with his towel thousands of times. (We went through a lot of face towels. The hotel must have thought I had a disgusting face-cleansing routine.)

A week later we made the trip back to the dental specialist, where they fit the titanium tooth over the nub of his bottom left canine tooth. The dentist told me it was a perfect fit and the glue needed to set for at least five days, so no tug and no toys. He said after that, though, he was full go for everything.

This timetable would push us into the middle of week five, and certification was going to be on the Tuesday of week six. Also, I couldn't use even the face towels for reward now. Only verbal and physical praise. The first time Mattis found a pseudo narcotic and I scratched his head and exuded a high-pitched "Good boi!" he was confused and looked around for a towel, a ball, or something to bite. But again, he seemed to understand and accepted my feeble reward system.

We made it to the day he was fully cleared to use his shiny new tooth. We started off that morning with a scent track. He dragged me along through the woods at a fast pace with the confidence that I would figure out how to navigate the same path he took (which was sometimes pushing through bushes, creeks, and under low-hanging branches). He went straight to my hiding classmate who, much to the surprise of Mattis, was holding out a tug toy for him to engage. It was like Christmas in August; he liked my praise, but he loved his toy! When he got rewarded with a ball after doing odor detection later in the day, he knew all was right with the world. But when he got to sink his teeth into a classmate wearing a bite suit, he realized it was not a perfect world—it was heaven!

As everything he had been learning was reintroduced to him in a full capacity, Mattis shifted into a higher gear of intensity. The instructors and my other classmates were confused as to how a dog that had been inactive for three weeks was crushing everything. I threw my hands up and said, "He's good!"

Certification Day

Certification day arrived. It was broken into five parts: obedience, detection, tracking, building search, and protection/apprehension work.

1. Obedience

Mattis and I walked into the testing area with him on a leash and ready to have fun. The evaluator told me to unleash him and have him sit by my side. A snap of the leash and it was like a switch went off and Mattis had read all the instructions for the test ahead of time. "Walk fast at a heel, now slow, now turn, now turn the other way, now run." Mattis pranced and stared at me for direction. I never said a word, just moved, and he reacted to every movement. "Have your dog lay down and stay there for three minutes." While walking, I dropped my right hand palm down from my chest to my beltline. Breaking stride instantaneously, Mattis put his belly on the ground and didn't flinch for three minutes. "Call him to your side and hook him up." As the instructor scribbled on his sheet, I heard him mutter "Wow!" under his breath.

2. Detection

For the detection portion of the certification there were six cars. Only four had odors in them, and once you identified the cars, the dog had to search the interior to find the odor inside the car. If your dog alerted to the wrong car, it was an automatic failure. If you went over the time limit, it was an automatic failure. Usually this was nerve-racking for the handler, but Mattis knew exactly where every single odor was as if it was a flashing light in complete darkness. The only difficulty he had was being inside the vehicles, because he is a humongous dog and each of the cars was a compact. Another pass with flying colors!

3. Tracking

Certification required at least a half-mile track, a cross track (another person to contaminate the tracking area by walking through), two surface changes, and at least three turns. Remember how I said Mattis tracks fast? The evaluator wasn't quite in the shape he needed to be to actually see the track. He caught up to us at the end of the track about five minutes after Mattis and I arrived.

4. Building Search

Mattis would have to search a building for a person in a bite suit hiding inside a closed room, alert me to his presence, then be rewarded with a bite. He sprinted to the door the decoy was hiding behind, lay down, looked at me (as if to say, "Watch this!"), then reached up with his paw and pushed the lever doorknob down, opening the door on his own and rewarding himself with a bite. I heard another wow from the evaluator amid the pain-filled screams of the decoy.

5. Protection and Apprehension

As it should be, protection and apprehension is the most difficult portion of the certification process. You have to show that your dog has the courage to engage when gunshots are going off (blanks are used). The gunshots might as well have been theme music for Mattis. In this test you send your dog on a decoy and recall him before he bites to simulate a suspect surrendering. Mattis pivoted on my word and sprinted to my side. You then approach the decoy and start to pat him down as if you are taking him into custody, and then the decoy attacks you. Your dog has to engage the decoy without a command to protect you. As soon as the decoy flinched, Mattis had him on his backside regretting his life choices.

———

The only dog to pass certification that day wasn't supposed to be a police dog, wasn't the dog I thought I had wanted, and was the only dog that had no odor training prior to the class. He had had only two weeks to train because he had been medically removed from the class, but he persevered and did an amazing job. I saw something in this dog and knew I couldn't give up on him. I could not wait to get him back to the police department in Alpharetta and watch the things he would do! That day and every day since, Mattis has made me look so much better than I am.

MY FIRST POLICE DOG, NIKO, IN 2012.

OUR FIRST PICTURE TOGETHER AFTER I SELECTED MATTIS. THE BOND STARTED INSTANTLY.

@k9_mattis

MATTIS LOOKING UP AT ME AND SHOWING A PEEK AT HIS TITANIUM TOOTH ON HIS BOTTOM LEFT CANINE.

MATTIS SITTING CALMLY NEXT TO HIS FAVORITE DECOY, CODY TALLENT.

MATTIS LOOKING FIERCE IN THE SNOW; THIS PHOTO WAS ONE OF MATTIS'S MOST FAMOUS.

MATTIS SHOWING OFF HIS FOCUS DURING A PUBLIC DEMONSTRATION.

TRYING TO MAKE TRAINING AS REALISTIC AS POSSIBLE; MATTIS IS LOCKED IN ON HIS TARGET.

MATTIS ON THE BITE OF A DECOY WITH A FULL MOUTH BUT CALM AND FOCUSED.

ONE OF MATTIS'S ALERTS LED TO THE
SEIZURE OF THAT STACK OF CASH.

TAKING TIME FOR A SELFIE
WITH MY BEST FRIEND.

MATTIS ROCKING A MUZZLE.

NO BETTER PLACE TO BE.

ON THE SET OF *LIVEPD* WITH DAN ABRAMS, SEAN LARSON, AND TOM MORRIS FROM JANUARY 3, 2020.

MATTIS BARKING WHILE WEARING HIS BULLETPROOF HARNESS.

SUN'S OUT, TONGUES OUT.

MATTIS'S WORK CRIB.

MATTIS TRAINING FOR
WATER OBSTACLES BEFORE
AMERICA'S TOP DOG.

BEHIND THE SCENES BEFORE
THE MEDIA PANEL FOR
AMERICA'S TOP DOG.

ON THE SET OF *AMERICA'S TOP
DOG* CHAMPIONS EDITION.

MATTIS ON THE SANTA MONICA
PIER. HE WAS ALWAYS BY MY
SIDE DURING THE MEDIA TOUR
FOR *AMERICA'S TOP DOG.*

SITTING IN THE KENNEL WITH MATTIS AS HE RECOVERED ON THE DAY AFTER HIS THIRTY-FOOT-RETENTION-WALL FALL.

THE FIRST PICTURE OF MATTIS AND I WHEN WE RETURNED TO HIT THE STREETS OF ALPHARETTA.

POSING IN THE MIDDLE OF THE ROAD LIKE RESPONSIBLE POLICE OFFICERS.

PRINCESS TEA PARTY WITH HARPER. MATTIS TOLERATES MANY SHENANIGANS!

MATTIS BEING SAVAGE.

STORM WATCHING ON AS
MATTIS GIVES A HIGH FIVE.

MODELING SOME SHADES
AND A HARNESS.

HAWK (MATTIS'S SON), MATTIS,
AND STORM READY TO GO
ON AN ADVENTURE.

SALUTING ON THE SET OF KATIE LINENDOLL'S
"YOUR HANDS" MUSIC VIDEO SHOOT.

MATTIS POST-RETIREMENT IN 2023 ON
THE SET OF KATIE LINENDOLL'S "EXTRA."

TRUST THE PLAN

*Trust in the LORD with all your heart and
lean not on your own understanding;
in all your ways submit to him, and
he will make your paths straight.*
—PROVERBS 3:5-6

Over the years, there have been a number of times when I stood on the cusp of something major in my life. When I held the letter that told me I was on academic probation from college. When I disembarked from the plane in San Diego to take the trip to Marine Corps Recruit Depot. When I knelt by the side of my bunk in the barracks in Camp Pendleton, with tears welling up, prayed to be forgiven, and surrendered my life to Jesus. When I saw my wife (then just an unknown beautiful girl) walk through the door to my apartment for the first time in her pleather jacket. When I cradled each of my kids as they were drawing their first breaths. And then when I stood in uniform with Mattis to my left for the first time. I knew some of those moments were significant as they were happening, others I did not. Standing next to Mattis for the first time in uniform was one of the former. I knew this dog was great, and I was overflowing with anticipation about the things he would do.

We had a strong unit with great dogs and great handlers who were open to learning together. I had three very clear goals for our unit:

1. Be excellent in training.
2. Be excellent in community relations.
3. Be excellent in deployments.

1. Training

The approach we took to training is one I stole from the martial arts world. The more I got into dog training, the more I realized how much it was like UFC in the early days. In UFC 1, each fighter represented a specific discipline, such as Brazilian jiujitsu, sumo, kickboxing, savate, boxing, shootfighting, wrestling, or tae kwon do. At first, each was trying to demonstrate that his discipline was the best fighting system. Eventually, smart fighters realized that if they learned as much as they could from each of the disciplines, then took what worked well for them and left out what didn't, they would be better than students who focused on only one discipline. They found the best instructors from each discipline and brought them into their camps. And that's how mixed martial arts was born.

I had been to dog-training schools and found that the trainers were very similar. In my early days as a handler I asked one trainer at a school where I should look to find more training as my career went on. He said, "Here. Don't go anywhere else. They will just confuse the dog." It felt like a scene out of an old kung fu movie on Saturday afternoons growing up, where he was pointing at me and saying, "Other kung fu is no good! Only this kung fu!"

One of the other obstacles you run into in police K9 training is that the most experienced handler is usually in charge of training. In our case, this was now me. I had only two years of handling experience and close to eight hundred hours of formal schooling. I'd trained for sixteen hours a month at the department, selected five dogs for police work, and trained firsthand about twenty dogs. That was a decent amount of experience, but when I compared it to my friend Cody Tallent, who had been a handler in the military for four years and now worked at a police K9 training facility every day, trained hundreds of dogs, trained 160 hours a month (at least), and selected hundreds of dogs, I didn't feel like me leading the training would make us the best. We needed someone with a lot of experience. Who was more qualified? Cody! Dog training was his main focus every day. He was the first person I brought in to make us better.

I brought in instructors from all over to teach us. We went to conferences for the purpose of finding passionate experts in each discipline and brought them into our working environment in Alpharetta. We made scenarios as realistic as possible. We found our threshold for failure, learned from the failure, and pushed past that threshold. There was energy and momentum building in our unit, and it was exciting!

2. Community Relations

In law enforcement, the community relations part of the job is often viewed as a necessary annoyance. Whenever a school requests a demonstration from a K9, usually the new guy gets tasked with it because no one else wants to. Our approach was very different. I made it clear—community relations were at least one-third of our job for a few reasons:

- People love dogs.
- We have dogs.
- People are interested in what dogs can do.
- Our dogs do awesome things (because we train hard).
- The people need us to protect them.
- We need the people to trust we will protect them and do what's right.

One of the other officers in my unit, Mike, was excellent at this long before I was in the unit. I had watched him interact with kids and adults, teaching and showing his dog Lekso's capabilities. He communicated with each audience in a way that they understood, and you could tell he loved his job. Because of Mike's efforts, people had a positive view of the police. He was the face of the department because of his willingness to engage with the public like he did. Unfortunately, he was leaving for a federal job, so the rest of us needed to get better.

I had recently taken a trip to SeaWorld for the first time and seen the orca show. When you break it down, orcas really do only a handful of tricks: they jump, they splash, and they drag a trainer around the pool on their fin. But what the show really does is tell a story as the orcas jump, splash, and drag. The story, when I went, was about a kid with a dream to be a trainer whose dreams come true and now he was riding in on the fin of his beloved friend, Shamu. He leapt off the fin to a platform. He took off his necklace with an orca symbol and passed on to a random kid in the audience not just the necklace but his dream. The crowd roared, Shamu splashed, and I learned.

There were four elements to the performance:

1. the story to evoke emotion;
2. the ability of the orca to perform;
3. the ability of the trainers to teach it;
4. the bond the trainer better have with an animal that is nicknamed "killer whale."

It takes a special person to jump into the water with an animal that is thirty feet long and weighs sixteen thousand pounds and that you hope is in a good mood. That's what people are really clapping for: the fascination with what the trainer and whale can do together and the special bond it takes to reach that level of performance.

This is what I always tried to highlight in demonstrations. My dog does amazing things (many more than Shamu), and we share a very special connection. I would volunteer for every demonstration there was. I would do impromptu public demonstrations in the mall, while walking around downtown, in parks. I knew there was a larger audience we could reach, so I proposed to our department the use of social media. I suggested Facebook because it was the only platform I was on and understood. They told me the dogs could have Instagram pages. I knew nothing about Instagram, but I took it and ran with it.

I learned as much as I could about what was good content on Instagram. At the time in 2015, it was about taking good pictures, writing good captions, and engaging with your audience. Luckily, I had a good-looking dog! I wrote the captions from his perspective and engaged with the community as much as I could. I was motivated to be excellent in community relations on a level that could reach a lot of people through the World Wide Internets. (It doesn't hurt that one of the other handlers challenged me to see who could get more followers.) People on the Insta (as I call it) were fascinated by Mattis, and his popularity grew quickly.

3. Deployments

A trained police dog costs around $14,000, and if you add in a titanium tooth, $19,000. A police vehicle with lights and sirens that is specially equipped with a heat alarm system and kennel for the dog is around $60,000. By the time you get the necessary collars, toys, leashes, and a bullet-proof vest for the dog, you are creeping up on $85,000. It costs a lot of money just to start a K9 unit. Deployments—when a unit is called on to do its job—are really where you show its worth.

I was eager to put Mattis to the test. The first week on the job we would find out whether he was worth it.

Mattis's narcotics detection was impressive, and we averaged around two arrests per shift we worked. This was an area of emphasis because there had been a recent epidemic of teenagers overdosing on heroin in the area. Our community was rightfully concerned. Mattis was doing his part to locate the drugs and where they were coming from. In most states, laws dictate that if property (houses, vehicles, cash, and things like that) is used in the commission of a crime, it can be seized. It depends on the direct correlation to the crime, the value of the property (is it worth seizing?), and the severity of the crime (in most cases it has to be a felony). With all of this, Mattis paid for himself in the first week he worked.

Most of that was just work ethic, though, getting out and doing the job. I wanted to see how good he really was. At the end of our first week I got an opportunity to put him to the test.

The First Track

It was a drizzly September afternoon. Everything outside was wet and the roads were slick. Traffic was thick, as it normally is around Atlanta. Our dispatch came across the radio that there was a smash-and-grab at the mall. (Suspects broke a display, stole items, and fled.) They gave a description of the vehicle the suspects had jumped into and the direction they were headed. I picked a direction on the freeway and started heading that way. Another officer happened to be in the area and located the suspects driving toward the freeway. The moment she turned on her lights and sirens, the vehicle raced away from her. We had a chase. My lights and sirens went on as I tried to get to the area faster to support the other officer.

Mattis knew what the sirens meant. You have to remember dogs learn by association quickly. Every time the lights had come on that week, he had gotten to get out and play a nose game that he adored. I heard him jump to his feet in the kennel and do happy circles.

Several things happen the moment a chase ensues. The initiating officer gives out pertinent information like the exact location, traffic conditions, and speed the suspects are traveling. In this case they were currently on surface streets, and the traffic was medium with speeds around seventy miles per hour in a thirty-five. The officer has to consider the severity of the crime and the need to apprehend the suspect versus the risk a chase poses to the rest of the public. This particular crime fell within the parameters of state law and our policy, and she felt at that moment she should pursue, so she did. The supervisor agreed with her over the radio.

I wasn't making much progress on the freeway because of the rain and heavier traffic. I knew she had another unit close to her, so I turned off my lights and sirens but continued south toward the chase. (Mattis was probably a little sad he didn't get to play a smelling game.) Just then the officer giving chase announced that the suspects had entered the freeway. She advised she was calling off the chase because the suspects were doing over one hundred, and the road and traffic conditions were making it danger-ous. It was a good decision but as always came with a feeling of disappointment. Dispatch gave out a BOLO (be on the lookout) to neighboring jurisdictions the vehicle might be traveling through.

I got off the freeway to find a place to set up an odor game for Mattis since he was probably feeling let down. It was raining, but I didn't care and knew Mattis wouldn't either. It was actually good to get him out in all the elements and train because one day he might have to work in less-than-ideal conditions. Little did I know that day was today.

As Mattis and I jumped out, dispatch announced that the city to the south of us had found a vehicle fitting the description of the suspects' spun out on the side of the free-way and wrecked. Mattis's paws had just hit the mud when I told him to jump back in. He had to be utterly confused. He never showed it, though, just trusted I knew what I was doing and obeyed.

The initiating officer and a supervisor made it to the scene well before I did. The supervisor gave me a call on the phone because he knew that I was heading that way. He told me some witnesses had seen the car spin out and get stuck in the mud on the side of the freeway, then they saw the suspects run from the scene. He said it was just a misdemeanor and that I didn't have to come if I didn't want to, especially because of the rain.

This supervisor had worked at the department for a while, and previously we'd had handlers who didn't like to use their dogs. They just enjoyed having dogs and ducking calls that other patrol officers had to go to. He knew they operated under the rules that an officer is never wet or hungry. I was different. I loved to work and I'm bald, so I don't mind getting wet. (As for hungry, I usually have snacks in the car.) I wanted to see what Mattis could do! I told the supervisor I was still coming.

I arrived at the scene of the spinout, which was about one mile north of the bridge that crossed the Chattahoochee River. The initiating officer gave me the details she had gathered from witnesses. She said they saw the suspects run toward the river and then disappear near a ditch about a quarter of a mile farther. This ditch ran along the freeway and had a drainage pipe that went under the freeway.

I walked back toward my vehicle to gather Mattis and the tracking gear. I was super excited that this was going to be our first track. I knew it would be difficult. We were going to have to start next to a busy freeway in the rain. Because of the cars zooming by, the odor they had left for us to track was being blown all over the place.

To me, tracking is the ultimate test of a good K9 team. The handler has to bring the dog to odor. The dog has to follow odor. The handler has to read the dog when he is on a good track and, if he's off, try to solve the puzzle as to where the dog lost the track and why. It is mentally and physically—especially with Mattis—demanding.

I slipped on my tracking gloves and grabbed Mattis's twenty-foot nylon tracking leash. I opened the door to his kennel, petted his head, and asked him if he was ready for this. I hooked him up to his obedience collar so he knew he was supposed to walk with me, not start working yet. He hopped out of the car and surveyed the scene. There were many sights and smells to take in. His head darted back and forth, processing what exactly his task was going to be.

As we walked by the supervisor, I asked, "Hey, can I get one?" He knew I was asking for a cover officer to come with me on the track. He replied, "Yup. Vinny, you want to go with him?" Vinny replied, "Yes sir!" I was glad. Vinny was new, but he was a good officer with a great attitude. I looked at Vinny and said, "He's fast, stay with us." Vinny nodded.

Of all the tracks I had done in my career, I couldn't remember any of my backup officers actually keeping up with us. Yet it was a vital role. As the handler, your focus is on the dog, and most of the time you are tracking criminals who are trying desperately to get away from the consequences of their behavior. In some cases, they may be willing to do harm to the officer coming after them. It is good to have at least one set of eyes scanning the area you are tracking rather than watching the dog. The physical demands of the track make it difficult, though, for some officers to keep up. But I had faith Vinny was up to the task.

I had Mattis lie down about ten feet from the rear of the spun-out vehicle the suspects had fled from. I switched the leash from the obedience collar around his neck to his tracking harness in the middle of his back. The moment he heard the snap of the metal clasp of the leash to the D ring on his harness, he bolted! The nylon leash hummed as it rubbed the leather on my tracking gloves. I gave him about seventeen feet of the twenty feet of the leash to get out in front, and we were off.

Mattis's head swung back and forth searching the air and ground for odors of people who had been in the area but were no longer there. He was looking for the scent profile of the only two people out of dozens of human odors that had fled the scene. When his head snapped toward the car, I knew he had solved the puzzle.

At a full sprint through the wet grass and mud and alongside a busy freeway, we headed south with Mattis in the lead, me holding on to keep up and Vinny trailing off to my side. We had reached the area of the ditch a quarter mile south from where we started, which is where the witnesses had last seen the suspects. The ditch went in two directions: southwest, wandering into a wood line, and east, directly under Georgia State Route 400. I was hoping for the wood line to the right, but Mattis made a hard left to the east into a three-foot-high concrete drainage pipe that traveled beneath the freeway. It was pitch black with water gently flowing through it, and Mattis was about ten feet into the pipe already.

As police officers, we carry about twenty-five pounds of gear on our bodies in the form of body armor, radios, medical equipment, ammo, and firearms (among other things). This equipment sometimes inhibits flexibility. Such was the case here as I tried to navigate the pipe. I was hunched over as best I could with my rigid body armor and was side skipping through the pipe as quickly as I could. Water and oil were dripping through the seams in the top of the pipe from the surface of the road above. The back of my body armor, and occasionally my head, were scraping across the rough concrete at the top of the pipe. I could hear the scurrying of small animals around my feet. (I was impressed Mattis gave the rats no mind but stayed on task.) Blood was running down my face from the scrapes on my head, and my back was on fire from the position I was holding to get through the pipe. I was already exhausted.

Finally, we approached the mouth at the other end of the pipe. Mattis stopped and appeared to be processing some sort of puzzle. I retracted the leash so I was standing with him outside the pipe and saw the dilemma. There was about a twenty-foot waterfall to the front of the pipe, impassable vegetation to the left, and to the right a muddy embankment that would require careful climbing or we would be falling the twenty feet to the rocky creek below.

Doubt started to creep in. I was tired, bloody, and in pain. All of this was just for shoplifting. I really wanted to quit. Mattis was standing on his hind legs sniffing the embankment to the right, and his tail was wagging. He was obviously having a blast. From his perspective, he was getting to play a game he loved with his best friend, and he had just located something that he was super excited about. There, stuck in thick mud, was the shoe of one of the suspects.

It was as if Mattis knew I wanted to give up, and he was showing me, *We can't stop. I know what I'm doing, just trust me.* Seeing the shoe gave me confidence in Mattis because this had already been one of the most demanding tracks I had been on, and this was his first ever "real" track. I whispered to Mattis, "Track," and he leapt up the embankment with ease. I carefully wormed my way up through the thick mud and helped Vinny up once I reached the top.

Now I was tired, wet, bloody, in pain, and muddy. But I had a refocused purpose to see what this amazing dog was capable of.

Mattis was moving at full sprint down a hill through a moderately wooded area to the creek bed below that the waterfall from the ditch fed into. I grabbed trees to maintain balance the best I could and at times slid on my backside because of the steep grade. As we approached the creek, I was worried because tracking through water was an advanced skill we really hadn't covered. The creek would carry odor the direction the water flowed. This could throw a dog off the track because where the suspects exit the creek and where their odor is carried may not be the same location. The tracking team would then have to scour the area to find the actual exit location.

Mattis hit the creek and ran right across it. I leapt from

slippery rock to slippery rock, still getting drenched, until I reached the other side. It took effort to take each step in the thick mud. Then he cut right back through the creek again, as did I. Then one more time. He then darted up a hill through heavy brush, dragging me along. I took branch after branch to the face and had to force my way through areas Mattis was able to nimbly navigate. He headed right back down to the creek again. For about three-quarters of a mile this continued. I was exhausted.

Mattis turned back up the hill with the thick brush again. I needed a break to rest and reassess the situation. I told Mattis to lie down so I could catch my breath. I looked over my shoulder to see if Vinny was still with us, not expecting to see him, but there he was. I was impressed with him. This had been a brutal track. Disappointment was creeping in. I couldn't be too upset, because a creek can throw off a seasoned dog. I knelt down just behind Mattis, leash grasped in my left hand, trying to catch my breath while also trying to figure out where we were. I was ready to call off the track and have someone come pick us up. We had tracked over a mile already, and I thought the creek had confused us enough. I saw a road off to our left and asked Vinny to go figure out what road it was.

Mattis began tugging at his leash and crawling to his right. It frustrated me even further. The weight of the failure of the track, my exhaustion, the pain, the mud, and the wetness were all hitting me in that moment, and now Mattis didn't want to obey me when I told him to lay down.

I growled a "nay" and was reaching up to take him off his tracking harness and put on his obedience collar when I saw what he was pulling toward. A shoe, a match to the shoe we had found by the pipe, stuck in the thick mud.

It was as if Mattis knew I was about to quit again, and in the moment I needed it most, he reassured me, *Trust me, Mark, I know what I'm doing. I know you can't see it, but I know the path they took. I can smell it. If you just listen and follow, I will get you there.*

I called to Vinny as he was walking toward the road, "Another shoe!" He came running back and we were off again. We were headed straight toward the Chattahoochee River, which was to the south about another half mile. We were moving at full speed through the woods when I saw two people walking north by the river back toward Georgia 400. I pointed them out to Vinny. Mattis made visual contact and we both took off at a full sprint.

The closer I got to the suspects, the more I could read in their body language and in their faces that they were spent. They were physically exhausted. One had a bare foot with a muddy sock dangling off the other. Once they caught sight of Mattis, I could tell that their will to flee was gone. There was a four-foot fence between us, and after they saw Mattis easily leap the fence, they put their hands up and lay down.

I struggled with the fence a tad more than Mattis did but made it over and approached the suspects. Vinny, who stayed with us the entire time, placed both suspects in handcuffs.

I was out of breath, wet, muddy, bloody—and ecstatic!

This track was more difficult than anything I had ever done before, in training or real life. Mattis exceeded every expectation I had with that track, and I almost missed it because I wanted to give up. I reached into the pouch on my belt that held Mattis's toy and tossed it to him with an enthusiastic "Good boy!" I followed up with scratches on his head and a hug.

I called on the radio and arranged for a patrol car to pick up the suspects on Georgia 400 North and another to pick up Vinny, Mattis, and me. As I walked up to the freeway, I thought about the track. The timing of finding both shoes in the moments I most wanted to quit was nothing short of providential. Of course I was able to see the obvious lesson: I needed to trust my dog. On a larger scale, it made me think about how God can see the beginning from the end. He knows what he is doing. He knows the path I need to take even if I can't see it. He says, "Just listen, follow, and I will get you there."

Life will beat you up. At times you will be exhausted, bloodied, wet, muddy, and frustrated. Press on. Don't quit. Every once in a while God will drop a shoe to give you confidence.

Later I made all the guys on the K9 unit run that same track. It became the first track I would run every dog team through when they came to the unit. I would always wait for a rainy day. I would leave clues so they wouldn't give up. I wanted them to grasp the lesson I learned: persevere, test your limits, and don't quit on your dog.

COMPLACENCY IS A KILLER

The complacency of fools will destroy them.
—PROVERBS 1:32

Mattis was showing me that he could handle anything I presented him with. He was such a good thinker. It was my job as his trainer to give him situations he had never been in before so he could learn how to successfully solve the puzzle. He would come up with solutions no one expected.

Problem-Solving

One day we were training in a recently closed department store in the mall. I had our decoy positioned between rows of shelving units in the middle of a pitch-black warehouse. This was to simulate a building search, as if a K9 team was dispatched to an alarm, saw some evidence it might be a legitimate break-in, and decided to use their K9 partner to help clear and locate any suspects still within the building. It was an interesting problem for the dogs because not only would they have to rely completely on their noses but they would also have to navigate the maze of shelves to actually get to the guy in the bite suit.

The instructions for the decoy were to remain silent and not move. In the majority of situations the dogs had been put through, they could use their nose, their hearing, and their sight to find and apprehend decoys. We were making it more complex to prepare for a possible real-life scenario where they might not be able to use their other senses and would have to rely on smell alone. If the first time they encounter a problem is in the real world, you can't be upset if they fail your expectations. As a trainer, you have to figure out what those situations may be and teach the dog to work through them.

The dogs could smell the decoy, but getting to the right row took a little while. If they chose the wrong row, they would be within two feet of the decoy but wouldn't be able to get to him. They would have to backtrack away from the strong odor to find another way. This is called free-shaping learning. You let the dog discover on their own without input from a handler.

Eventually the dog learns it has to use a combination of skills to locate the decoy. At the beginning of the exercise the handler tells the dog to do an area search to locate and apprehend a suspect within. Because of the obstacles, the dog learns that it also needs to use tracking (smelling the ground to find the exact route the decoy took) to locate their reward.

It is a fun exercise to listen to. You hear heavy sniffing, the clickity-clack of the dog's nails on the cement, and confused pauses as the dog tries to figure out how to get to its most prized reward, the human chew toy. Minutes later, after trial and error, you hear a scream of pain from the decoy. (Yes, it hurts to get bit when you wear the bite suit, but also the scream is a reward for the dog. The decoy turns into not only a human chew toy but also a squeaky chew toy, which is even better.) Dog after dog went and solved the problem as expected. It usually took them around three to five minutes to figure it out . . . until the last dog, Mattis.

I knelt beside Mattis, who was obediently lying, and gave our required commands. "Police department K9 unit. Make yourself known, or I will release my dog and he will bite you!" Mattis was silent but excited. Because of his remarkable nose, he already knew that there was someone inside this great expanse of darkness. Even though he was about a hundred yards away, he could smell the sweat, the soaps, the foods, and the fear emanating from the guy in the bite suit. (It is always a little nerve-racking getting bit in the dark because you don't know when exactly it's going to happen and where you may get bit.) He could also smell the bite suit itself. Mattis crawled forward in anticipation of the word that would release him to begin the hunt. I whispered in his right ear, "*Revier.*" This is the command that tells Mattis to use his nose to find the person inside, then apprehend him. He disappeared into darkness.

I heard his nails digging into the concrete and then a thud, followed by a series of similar thuds and a scream of surprise and pain, but it had only been about fifteen seconds! We flipped on the warehouse lights and sprinted to the location where the decoy was. This took probably twenty to thirty seconds. At the end of the row, I could see the decoy and Mattis's head popping out of the shelving unit about five feet off the ground. I gave Mattis the command to release and rewarded him with his ball, which he enthusiastically chomped down on while prancing about.

I asked the decoy what happened. He told me he heard Mattis go down a row in the distance and then jump up onto a shelf. He said he then jumped from shelf to shelf (in the dark) straight toward him at about head level. The decoy said, "I know I was supposed to be still, but he was coming at me head level, so I threw my arm up to intercept him."

The other handlers, the decoy, and I were all astounded. This was not what I had planned. This was not the lesson I wanted to teach Mattis. I laughed because he'd solved it in a manner I hadn't considered, and in a more efficient way. This type of Mattis solution became commonplace at every training session. Throw a complex problem at him and just watch him with wonder as he comes up with a solution. We never knew what it was going to be, but we knew it was going to be grounded in determination, athleticism, and efficiency.

Engaging with Social Media

I began to share some of our training sessions live on Instagram. People enjoyed the inside peek into our training. I would engage the audience as much as possible and show them the high standard we trained to, the amazing dogs, and the handlers who loved their jobs so much. Sharing the training sessions was in keeping with our philosophy in two areas: First, it kept us training at a high level since we knew people were watching; and second, it satisfied our desire to be excellent in community relations. It helped that we had amazing dogs and some really fun handlers who enjoyed being around each other.

The sharing of our training sessions led me to begin a series of videos I called the Door Popper Game. This game wasn't taught at most K9 handler schools, but it was an important skill. A K9 deputy in Mississippi had been ambushed by three men and dragged into the woods, presumably to die. His dog was still in the SUV, but the deputy was able to hit his door popper. The K9 sprang into action and saved the deputy's life. You can see how valuable this skill can be.

It is an easy skill to teach your dog. You stand right outside the door, hit the release, encourage your dog to come, then reward him when he does. You gradually increase the distance you are away from the vehicle and eventually start hiding from plain view of the dog so that he has to use his nose to find you. I would also add in other complications like water crossings and crowds of people. We played this game daily.

For the "gram," I would go live and run away from my SUV. I would try to hide in places that would be difficult for Mattis to find me. I hid in ditches, in dumpsters, and on top of shipping containers, to name a few. I would ask viewers to guess how long it would take Mattis to find me. The door popper had a range of about two hundred yards, so most of the time he would find me in about twenty seconds.

Mattis was becoming a hit on Instagram. In addition to training sessions, I posted handsome photos of Mattis with captions posted from his perspective and his life at home with my family. It was amazing that this absolute machine of a working dog would go home and let my one-year-old daughter lie on him. From time to time, I may have thrown a princess dress on Mattis and had him participate in tea parties with my daughter. He is such a tolerant dog!

There were definitely some detractors as well. I took some criticism from other handlers and trainers because they believed I was making my dog soft. There are some schools of thought in the police dog training world that the dog is to be treated as a tool. It stays in a kennel, it goes to work, it trains, it deploys, and then it goes back in the kennel. The only human interaction it has is with its handler. This is a good idea for some dogs. The K9 unit is one of the highest-liability units a department can have. So this is the "if they aren't ever around people, they can't accidentally bite someone" philosophy.

My philosophy in training was different. Mine was the "get them around as many people as possible and teach them how to act and who they are supposed to bite" philosophy. (Not a very catchy title for my philosophy.) As a dog trainer, something I learned was that you try to expose your dog to as many scenarios as possible so that it is never surprised. If it is surprised, there is no telling how it might react.

I also understand where the criticism comes from. Some handlers out there just like the status of being in a K9 unit. They have highly social dogs and love to show them off, but when it comes time to work, they aren't worth much.

That's why the criticism actually fueled me. It made me want to train harder. Plus, I knew something they didn't know. I knew Mattis and what he was capable of. I knew how special this dog was and I knew he was going to make an impact. I knew he could do both.

Muzzle Training

As I studied, I learned that one of the major problems a lot of dogs have is engaging on their first bite. I had actually seen this in action years ago with a dog sent on his first bite. The dog was given the command to go apprehend. He took off at a full sprint, catching up to the suspect quickly but then running in circles around the suspect while hesitantly leaping on his hind legs. With more encouragement from the handler, the dog nipped at the suspect but never fully latched on. The suspect fell and we were able to take him into custody. This happens a lot more than you might think.

The issue here is that the dog is being presented with something he never has before: a subject to bite who isn't wearing a bite suit. In training, every time that dog was sent to apprehend a suspect, the suspect was wearing a bite sleeve or bite suit. Now the dog sees something new and doesn't know how to react.

Now, the situation that I had seen had worked out okay, but it also could have been a disaster. The suspect could have gotten away—or worse. Think back to the event in Mississippi; if that brave dog hadn't done what he was supposed to do, the life of the officer would have been lost.

This was the kind of thing we had to train for. I didn't want our dogs to fail when the handler needed them to act. The easy way to train for this would be to have the decoy wear no protective gear and just get bitten. I don't think we would get many volunteers for that. Another way was to take away the dog's ability to cause damage with its teeth but still attempt to apprehend a suspect with no protective gear. Sounds like a better option. Enter muzzle training.

Mattis wasn't a fan of muzzle training. It's not that he didn't like the muzzle. I had worked with him, so he liked wearing it. He didn't like the idea of me telling him to go bite someone when I took away his ability to bite. I couldn't blame him. I wasn't frustrated; I actually saw it as a sign of intelligence.

I had to figure out a way to give Mattis the mental picture of no equipment on a decoy while still encouraging him to engage. A company made a prosthetic-looking forearm and hand attached to a baseball bat that I thought would be perfect. We hid a decoy inside a wooden box with a door. The dogs would smell the human odor they were looking for and then the decoy would expose the fake arm. Most of the dogs were confused when the arm was presented, but eventually they engaged it. Mattis, on the other hand, had no confusion. The second he had access to any part of the baseball-bat arm, he clamped down on it, ripping it from the grasp of the decoy inside the box. He then spit out the arm (that he had presumably ripped off in his mind) and lunged to get inside the box so he could clamp down on another appendage. He got it. I was pretty sure he wasn't going to have any issue with engaging someone not wearing equipment.

Plan for the Worst, Hope for the Best

The most common call a police officer goes on that turns out to be nothing is an alarm call; 99.999 percent of calls are false alarms. It happens for different reasons: store employees forget the code; cleaning crews don't know the code; homeowners forget they set the alarm; even bad weather can set off alarms. All of those false alarms can lull officers into a sense of complacency. But it is vitally important that we never take them lightly.

One night, the shift I was working was getting slammed. Our dispatch announced on the radio that they had an alarm, and a key holder (a term we use to describe a person who is listed as a contact with the alarm company) was on the way. I wasn't too far away, so I headed that direction. There were no other units available, so a lieutenant was responding with me.

When you pull up to a potentially dangerous call, you never pull up right in front of the property. It puts you in a really bad position if a bad guy is waiting on you. I parked just down the street from the house we got the call on. I saw a person on the front porch about to open the door with a phone in her hand. I wasn't concerned that this was possibly a criminal because a look of relief crossed her face when she saw me. It was the key holder. I waved her over to find out anything she knew and to keep her from walking into the house.

She explained that this was her parents' house, and they were out of town. She also mentioned that there was damage to the back door, but she thought the damage was old. I told her I was going to wait for my backup officer and then we would check the house before she went in. I then asked her to wait over by my car until we knew that it was safe.

I quickly walked around the outside of the house and checked for signs of forced entry. I saw that the glass in the back door had been broken above the door lock. I heard the lieutenant call over the radio that he was on scene. I told him to meet me at the rear where we could see the back door, and I explained the situation to him before asking him to wait while I got Mattis from the vehicle.

I went over the details in my head. There were signs of forced entry, but the key holder thought it had been like that before. When an alarm goes off, the alarm company is alerted, then they contact a key holder before contacting the police (usually about ten minutes after the initial alarm). If it was a burglary, they likely heard the key holder about to open the door and took off out the back. My conclusion was that it was highly unlikely there was anyone inside.

I hooked Mattis up to his twenty-foot leash. I was going to use a fishing-type technique where Mattis would search to the end of his leash in front of us. If he found something, he would bite down and I could pull it to where I was, just like fishing.

One of the most amazing things Mattis does began the moment I got him out of the car. He saw the leash, so he knew he would be searching for human odor. The key holder was standing by my car, so he knew that wasn't who he would be looking for. He saw the lieutenant standing outside the house, so he also eliminated him from the scent profile he would be searching for. As he lie down by the back door, he began to analyze the smells the world and the house had to offer. He knew something that the key holder, the lieutenant, and I did not. His highly sensitive vomeronasal organ could detect fear coming from within the house. He could smell a unique scent profile permeating the house like a beacon in a dark room. We were oblivious to all of this.

In training scenarios, I typically know where the decoy is. It is Mattis's job to find it and it is my job to read him, so I know his behaviors. I usually know more, but in this case he knew more.

Before I send a dog into a structure on a search-and-apprehend command, it is important to make sure that anyone inside is given the chance to surrender. I reached through the broken windowpane and opened the door, then yelled into the house, "Police department K9 unit. Make yourself known or I will release my dog and he will bite you!" Silence. No response.

Again I yelled, "Police department K9 unit. Make yourself known or I will release my dog and he will bite you!"

Still silence.

"Final warning. Police department K9 unit. Make yourself known or I will release my dog and he will bite you!"

I unholstered my duty weapon and leaned down to Mattis and whispered, "Revier." That was his cue that he was free to use the amazing God-given locating tool in his nose: find the threat within the building and neutralize it. He lunged into the house without fear. He was on a mission. The leash hummed as it was being let out of my gloved left hand. The end of the leash had a knot in it so I would be able to grasp it and keep it from slipping away. As I gripped the knot, Mattis didn't slow. He pulled me into the house.

Usually Mattis would search methodically through each room to clear a structure. This time he was driving hard into the house away from where we entered, bypassing other rooms. I told the lieutenant, "Clear behind me, he smells something!"

Mattis went straight down the only hallway in the ranch-style single-level house. He veered to the left into a bedroom and lie down at the threshold of the doorway in a diagonal manner, facing to the right side of the bedroom into the blind corner and closet.

He was alerting me to the presence of the suspect and I knew it, but I couldn't see the threat. My heart began to pound as I choked up on the leash. My lieutenant got to my position, and I told him, "He's right there!" as I gestured into the room. It was a super tight fit in the bedroom because of a queen-size bed that took up about 70 percent of the room. I angled my way into the room and saw a pile of clothes in front of an empty closet. Mattis was fixated on the pile.

My heart went from what had to be an audible pounding to an abrupt stop as I scanned the pile of clothes and noticed a bloodshot, brown human eye staring up at me. He was no more than seven feet away from me, and Mattis was focused and ready to act. I gave more commands. "You in the pile of clothes, show me your hands or you will get bit!" No response. I tried twice more. Still no response.

I wondered if the suspect just thought I was bluffing or if he was setting up for a counterattack. His entire body was covered with clothes, so I couldn't see whether he was armed. A burglary offender met the criteria for an apprehension by dog bite. I also wondered how Mattis would perform. This was an interesting puzzle. Mattis couldn't see the offender, only smell him. I had never run a scenario like this where the dog had to jump in blindly, but it was the right decision. I whispered, "Stellen."

Mattis dove headfirst into the pile of clothes. There

was a scream, and then the sound of a wooden baseball bat clanking about on the hardwood floor. Mattis pulled back with his jaw clamped down on the right arm of the offender, and he kicked the bat the offender had been holding on to— he'd been waiting for us to approach so he could attack. Mattis acted too swiftly and strongly for the offender to get a swing off. He was now fully exposed in the hallway. With the incentive of the pressure from the bite, the previously uncooperative offender was now more than willing to comply with every command. I was able to secure the offender in handcuffs, and I told Mattis "*Los*" (the Dutch command for let go), as I dangled a ball as a substitute for what he was currently engaged with. Mattis happily let go of the offender, chomped down on his ball, and pranced about.

"What do you think, Lieutenant?"

"Wow, that could have been bad! Good dog!"

Man, I loved this dog.

I ran through the scenario in my head of what it could have looked like if we hadn't had Mattis. It could have been very bad. If he hadn't sniffed out the burglar immediately and alerted us to his presence, the burglar would have had the tactical element of surprise when we entered the room. The bat and the tight space would have made it a brutal fight, and it could have escalated quickly. Mattis protected us and probably saved the burglar's life in the process.

This was Mattis's first bite and he executed it flawlessly. I was glad I had a dog that was tuned in, focused, and ready, because I was anything but. When I first approached the situation, I was complacent, assuming this was like the 99 percent of all alarm calls. My complacency could have gotten the other officer and me hurt. The lesson slapped me in the face: expect the worst and hope for the best.

The next training day, I put on the bite suit and hid under a pile of clothes for each of the dogs in the unit. I brought up my almost fatal mistake of being complacent. If it happened to me, it could happen to the other K9 officers. I've heard it said that the moment you think you are good or have arrived is the moment you start sliding into mediocrity. I wanted us to be a unit that was always striving to learn more and get better.

GOD WORKS FOR THE GOOD

We know that in all things God works for the good of those who love him, who have been called according to his purpose.
—ROMANS 8:28

Remember the story I told you about Mattis in the first lesson? I left you on a bit of a cliffhanger. After Mattis jumped over a thirty-foot-high wall, I knew that he was seriously injured. I rushed him to the vet as fast as I could. The only way I can describe the drive to the emergency vet was that my body was on autopilot while my mind raced between the events that had occurred, the worst-case scenario, and simple prayers asking the Creator of the universe to save my dog. Weak whimpers came from the kennel as I thought about what I could have done differently to prevent this whole situation.

If I had just ignored the strange lane change that car had made. That's how it all started. I had just turned south on North Point Parkway to head to my favorite gyro spot. The silver BMW made an odd, abrupt lane change that drew my attention. Unbeknownst to the driver, I had no idea they had just robbed somebody.

Please, God, don't let him die!

If the BMW hadn't busted through the red light in heavy traffic, I would not have attempted to make the traffic stop. I had run the tag because of the lane change, and it came back to a rental. Nothing too suspicious about a rental. Sure, they didn't use their blinker when they changed lanes, but if I took the time to pull over everyone who didn't use the turn indicator, I would set a record for the number of traffic stops.

Move, cars! Don't you see the lights and hear the siren? Get out of the way!

If they hadn't pulled a U-turn when they were getting away from me. I mean, who does that in a car chase? You begin to get away from the pursuing vehicle and then pull a U-turn and head straight back toward it and let it catch back up?

I reached back into the kennel. "You're going to be all right, buddy. Hang in there, please hang in there!"

If the car hadn't crashed into a parking lot where another officer was staged. How unlucky can a couple of criminals get? The chances of them pulling into that parking lot, with a cop there disabling their best chance at getting away, has to be the same chances as winning the lottery.

A few more minutes; we are almost there.

If the suspect hadn't jumped over the wall. He saw me and he saw Mattis. Why didn't he just give up or look before he jumped?

Those thoughts were fleeting. A series of events had unfolded that put me in the right place at the right time to catch people breaking the law. That's my job. The questions that haunted me came next.

Why did I hit the door popper? I knew the answer, but it still didn't change my regret for pushing it. I hit the door popper because people are usually much more likely to give up when they see a dog—especially one the size of Mattis. When someone looks at me, they see a short guy with small legs they think they can probably outrun or take in a fight. There was no way of knowing how the events might turn, and having Mattis present usually made me more prepared for whatever might happen.

Why didn't I leash him up? If I had had him on leash when he jumped, I could have pulled him back up. I knew the answer to this as well. The moment I put the Tahoe into Park, I saw the suspect running directly toward me. In the time it would've taken me to leash up Mattis, the suspect would have gotten away. Even if I had gotten it on quickly, it was likely that with Mattis's momentum as he jumped, I would have been yanked down the thirty-foot retaining wall and severely injured, or worse.

As the scene replayed in my mind, the only lens I could see the events in was that all of it happened because of a series of poor decisions on my part. My mind was automatically going to the worst possible outcome, and I couldn't help but blame myself. I believe this was the Enemy hurling accusations at me, so I relied on a simple prayer over and over throughout the evening: *Please, God, save him!*

As I pulled up to the emergency vet clinic, there was a gurney with a technician standing by, waiting for us. The tech was small in stature, and I knew she would have difficulty picking Mattis up. I was sure she had done it a hundred times or more, but Mattis was big, injured, and scared. More than her ability to lift, I was worried about him being compliant. I threw the Tahoe into Park and jumped out. I opened the kennel door and Mattis attempted to stand, but the pain was too great. He crumpled back onto the rubber floor mat. I scooped him up with an arm in front of his front paws and the other tucking his tail around his backside and hugged him tight to my chest. I remember thinking this might be the last time I hugged him, and my eyes began to water. I stayed on mission and laid him on the gurney.

The doctor was holding the front door for us, and I explained the circumstances as we pushed Mattis into the back of the office. Most vets don't allow you to go into the back with your dog. I told the vet that they would probably need my help in keeping Mattis calm. He's an amazing dog, but I had learned that he hated being left alone at the vet. I had boarded him at his regular vet one time and the techs had told me no one could go near him. If I were to leave him with the emergency vet, he might hurt the tech, the vet, or himself even more.

The doctor processed the information as I conveyed the events, and he decided Mattis needed X-rays. I transferred Mattis onto the X-ray table, which was slippery and barely large enough for a dog his size. The techs gave me a lead apron to cover myself, and in between each shot I placed my head on his and whispered, "You're going to be okay, buddy, you're going to be okay," and kissed his head. Mattis's eyes just locked onto me, and I understood his gaze to mean *I'm hurting, I'm scared, but I trust you. Please help me.* There were a hundred things happening around him that had to be confusing to a dog, but in that moment I was his whole world and he never took his eyes off me.

A few minutes later the doctor clicked through the images on the computer that displayed the X-rays. He looked at me and the vet tech and blurted with urgency, "We need to get him into surgery now! He is bleeding internally." Those words hit me like a two-by-four. From my limited knowledge of first aid, I knew that an aortal bleed could kill you in a matter of minutes. I didn't know where Mattis was bleeding internally, but I knew that it couldn't be good. I lifted Mattis against my chest, followed the vet tech into the operating room, and laid Mattis down on the cold, stainless steel operating table. I held his head and stroked his fur as they gave him an IV and he drifted off to sleep.

In Surgery

I had so many questions, but I could tell the vet was focused on the task in front of him. If he was going to save Mattis, I needed to get out of the way and let him do what he was trained to do. I walked to the area at the front of the office where other people were sitting and waiting on their pets and who were, I am sure, equally as concerned about their animals. I decided to go out to my Tahoe, which was still parked by the curb in a fire lane in front of the office. I jumped in and pulled into a parking spot, threw the car into

Park, laid my head on the steering wheel, and, with tears in my eyes, started praying.

God, I know he's just a dog, but to me he is so much more. You know how much time I spend with him, more than any person on the planet. He is my best friend. I know that everything is within your control, and nothing happens without your providence. Guide the hands of the doctor and give him wisdom. I understand your plans are higher than mine, but please let my plan align with yours, and let Mattis be okay. In Jesus' name, amen!

It was out of my hands, as it always was. I unstrapped my ballistic vest and tossed it onto the passenger seat before I walked back toward the clinic. I knew it was going to be a long night, so I called my wife and let her know what was happening. I felt completely helpless as I settled into a chair in the corner of the waiting room and allowed myself to process the ups and downs of the emotional roller coaster that the day had been.

Most of the ups came from my phone buzzing with text messages from friends, family, and colleagues offering prayers and thoughts. The downs came from me beating myself up for getting into the situation in the first place and dwelling on the darkest possible outcome. I knew God was in control, but I didn't know what his plan was.

Several people stopped by the clinic to console me during this time and show support for Mattis: the lieutenant who was currently on duty, the patrol commander, a captain—a former marine like me. They all offered some encouraging words. A fire chief who has always been a great example of leadership when we shared calls for service together stopped by, and so did the deputy chief of the police department—a good man who cared genuinely about the people in the department. Finally, a state senator I had seen in passing but never met showed up. Without any cameras or accompaniment, he showed up to let me know he and his wife were lifting us up in prayer.

Whenever there is a significant incident, something called a command page goes out to command staff and other interested parties (like the senator). It meant the world to me that those people read that Mattis was injured and showed up. My wife was checking in regularly, and even though she often joked about what a pain in the butt Mattis was, deep down I knew she loved him and it had to be driving her crazy that she wasn't able to be with me. Although I was hardly emotionally stable, their presence and concern brought comfort and helped pass the time—time that felt like torture to me. The quiet. The not knowing what was happening in the back of the clinic. Minutes seemed like hours, except when I had someone with me offering wisdom, encouragement, or prayer.

In the quiet moments my thoughts would play cruel games with me. I would go from thinking how amazing Mattis was at his job to accusing myself with thoughts like *You just ruined him! He will never be the same! Why did you hit the door popper? Why didn't you leash him up? How could you let him fall? Why didn't you jump?* More tears.

There was a door on the left side of the lobby with a black-and-white plastic sign that read Employees Only, and all I wanted was for that door to open so I could learn what was happening. Eventually I saw the handle of the door turn, and I jumped to my feet, anticipating news of some sort. As it opened, I could see it was the vet. I knew the words he spoke would have an impact on my life forever, so I took a deep breath, grabbed the armrest on the chair closest to me, and braced myself for what he had to say.

He started by saying, "Mattis had a lacerated liver." I didn't like how he used the past tense.

But then he said, "I really can't believe what happened."

I nodded, hoping it would encourage him to get to the point.

"By the time we got to where he was bleeding from, it had stopped on its own."

Just as I started to feel a sense of relief, he continued. "But we did find something else concerning."

My heart sank.

"When we looked at the X-rays, we saw something in his stomach and pulled out half of a tennis ball."

Immediately I felt relief. Yes, tennis balls can be dangerous. Mattis had destroyed a tennis ball or two before. I knew the tennis ball was not what caused him to collapse. "So he's going to be okay?"

"Miraculously, yes! I don't know how the bleeding stopped, but it did."

I knew. My department had posted on Facebook about

Mattis's fall, others had shared with friends and family, and my wife had posted something on our Instagram. There were thousands of people praying for my best friend, and the Bible says the prayer of the righteous is powerful and effective. God was in control. God answered. An overwhelming sense of relief and gratitude came over me for the vet and for those who showed up, called, texted, and prayed. So many people shared my burden when I was helpless, and God showed up.

I asked what was next and the vet told me Mattis was sleeping. I asked if I could see him and he said not until the morning. I made the decision to go home and get cleaned up. I am sure they were happy with that decision because wearing a ballistic vest while chasing people through the woods creates quite a significant stink.

Recovery

After a sleepless couple of hours and a much-needed shower, I drove back to the emergency clinic to ask if I could just be with Mattis. The staff at the vet clinic were incredibly understanding and compassionate. They allowed me full access. They had Mattis in the largest kennel and had placed a dog bed and blankets inside. It was about three feet high, three feet wide, and five feet deep. As I approached, I saw Mattis lying on his side in a deep sleep.

Mattis's nose twitched as it recognized a familiar, and

apparently important, smell. He slowly raised his head and turned toward me. When his eyes made it to my frame, they confirmed what his nose had already revealed: it was me. He struggled to his feet and his tail swayed from side to side. Then he lay back down as his body refused to cooperate with what his mind wanted to do.

Everything about Mattis, up until this point, had screamed powerful, resilient, and confident. Now I saw a weak, scared, and dependent dog. His belly was shaved and sported a foot-long incision with silver staples keeping it shut. I opened the kennel and sat down inside. Mattis again struggled to his feet and stepped gingerly toward me before lying down again and placing his head on my legs. Feeling the weight and warmth of his head is one of the greatest memories I have. I put in headphones and stroked his massive head. He fell asleep, and at times I did as well. For the first time since he'd fallen, I felt at peace.

The plan was that I would take Mattis to my regular vet when they opened on Monday morning so they could evaluate him and come up with a course of action. By Monday morning the sedatives had worn off enough that he could walk to the vehicle, but pain was keeping him from leaping up into his kennel. He looked up to me, silently requesting my help. I squatted down and gently lifted him into the kennel, and we made the drive to the regular vet with his medical records from the procedure in hand.

Our vet reviewed the records and listened to how Mattis sustained the injuries. He explained they wanted to observe

Mattis for two or three days before sending him home with me. I wouldn't be able to remain with him just because of the business of the office and the space he would be in. I didn't like that we would be apart, but I understood the reasoning. I gave him a hug and some head scratches as I left the office and headed home to wait.

Ten minutes later, as I pulled into my driveway, my phone began to buzz. The caller ID showed Alpharetta Animal Hospital. I slid my finger across the screen to answer the call, wondering why they would be calling this soon.

"You have to come back!"

"Oh no, why?"

"Mattis won't calm down since you left. He is going to rip his stitches out!"

"I'll be there in ten minutes."

My wife jumped into the car with me, and we headed back to the animal hospital. The vet met me in the lobby and explained he thought it would be best if Mattis went home with me. I was ecstatic at this news. Apparently Mattis did not understand the reasoning behind our being apart. While I acquiesced to the vet's request, Mattis pitched a fit until he got his way!

Mattis was still weak and still in pain. In his own way he explained to the vet something I could not:

Doctor, Mark is my best friend. He is the only being on this planet who has been consistently there for me since I was born. We spend every waking moment together. If he goes somewhere, I go with him. I usually protect him, but now I need him to protect me. I'm hurt, I'm confused, and he is my world. I need to be with him.

The door swung open as Mattis dragged the vet tech through the hallways. His whole body swayed from side to side from the energy in his tail, which was expressing happiness as dogs do. I fell to my knees as Mattis spun in circles, whapping me in the face with his tail and then coming around to do the same with his tongue. He repeated the cycle a few times. His excitement level proved he knew he was coming home with me.

As I lifted Mattis into the back of our SUV, I felt a great sense of comfort. I didn't know whether he would ever be able to serve as a police dog again, but I knew he would be going home with me. I didn't care if it meant I never handled another dog; he would always be with me.

As Mattis recovered over the next few days and weeks, I started to realize the impact of his heroism. I read all the comments on the department's post, and each one brought me a sense of gratitude. So many people cared enough not only to comment but also to lift Mattis up in prayer. To this day I believe the reason he is alive is because of all those prayers. It also showed me that the investment we had made in the community was very worthwhile.

Media outlets began reaching out to me about Mattis's story. I had never considered how remarkable the whirlwind of events was because I was so caught up in the uncertainty of his well-being. My loyal partner and best friend fearlessly pursued a suspect over a treacherous thirty-foot embankment and captured him peacefully despite sustaining life-threatening internal injuries. Then with determination and focus that overrode his pain, Mattis pursued the other suspect, who wisely chose to surrender. It was only after completing his mission, giving his all, and acting with unwavering bravery and determination that he collapsed.

The captain who had taken the time to stop by and check on Mattis at the vet called to tell me that he was going to forward an email that I would want to read. When the notification hit, I couldn't believe who it was from: none other than General James "Mad Dog" Mattis, the legendary marine my best friend was named after. I was overcome with emotion because here was a man I held in the highest regard taking the time to reach out through various channels to get a letter to me (and, more importantly, to Mattis). Filled with gratitude, I responded to convey my appreciation. Astonishingly, I received a direct reply from the general himself minutes later. As if it were possible, my respect for the type of leader and person General Mattis was grew.

Officer of the Year

While I was blown away by the ever-growing impact of Mattis's actions, I was still concerned about whether he would ever be able to work as my partner again. Mattis did not share this concern. Two things drove him to get back to work with me: he loved working and he loved being with me. After a week of watching me leave to patrol without him, he decided that was enough. He was back but only in a single-purpose narcotics-detection capacity. It remained to be seen whether he would recover enough to perform the more physical parts of the job, like tracking and apprehension. If nothing else, I knew I was going to have my best friend back at work with me.

Even though I was thrilled to have Mattis back, there was one thing that I was afraid of: that Mattis might have developed post-traumatic stress associated with heights or performing tasks associated with pursuing suspects. Dogs are associative learners, and what he went through could have set up a very negative association with some of his job functions. That would be the end of his ability to track and apprehend. As he healed, I began to test how he reacted to heights. There didn't seem to be any negative effects. I began to work in pursuing suspects, and again, he was the same magnificent dog he had always been: confident, strong, and happy.

I loved this dog, but I still wasn't sure whether, in a real situation, the trauma he had gone through might cause him to hesitate. As we began to get back into our routine of working hard, training hard, and interacting with as many people as we could to build bridges in the community, one of my supervisors pulled me aside one day and told me I needed to go to our annual awards banquet. I had an inkling Mattis might receive some recognition for what had happened. I told my wife, and she invited my sister and parents to come as well.

Mattis was well behaved but probably bored during the ceremony. The event was held inside a church. He lay quietly at the end of the pew where I sat. I thought he might join in when the deputy director performed an interesting vocal solo of "Amazing Grace," but he merely picked up his head and looked puzzled during the performance. The director of public safety took the pulpit and began the awards portion. He led by reading a summation of the events Mattis had been through in October, adding that he acted with bravery and valor while sustaining life-threatening injuries in the line of duty. Then he gave him the departmental Purple Heart. I took great pride in my dog being recognized for his heroism and perseverance. Those in attendance clapped as I walked Mattis up to receive his medal. I pinned it on his vest. A few pictures were snapped, and we took our seats.

The director started reading off the next award: Officer of the Year. I was still admiring the dangly medal on Mattis's vest when I heard the words "Officer Mark Tappan and K9 Officer Mattis." Mattis and I walked back up and were presented with a nice glass award on top of an engraved wooden base for Officer(s) of the Year. More pictures were snapped.

Mattis and I walked back to our seats next to my family in the second row. Mattis circled and lay down in the aisle. The director's aide-de-camp moved a three-foot table center stage and placed on it a heavy object covered by a cloth. He was wearing white gloves so he wouldn't smudge the award beneath the cloth.

The director began to explain the Director's Award, saying that it was for an officer who demonstrated excellence in character, leadership, and service. He gushed about how this was a special award because he alone made the decision about who should receive the honor. He said that the department had never done this before, but he could think of no officer that represented the award better than Mattis.

We rose for a third time and walked onto the stage. Mattis was oblivious to the honor. He was more confused about why we kept making the thirty-foot journey to the stage and then back to the pew over and over again. I was not oblivious, however; I was overwhelmed with pride and humbled to be associated with this amazing dog. The cloth was removed from the award, revealing a two-foot-tall bronze eagle with an inscription on the base for Mattis. I hoisted the award and nodded to the audience.

As we headed back to our spot, the lesson was clear to me. Through the confusion, trials, panic, and pain, our circumstances were never outside of God's control, and he, as he promised, worked for the good. I didn't realize how much good was still to come.

BE STRONG AND COURAGEOUS

Be strong and courageous.
—DEUTERONOMY 31:6

When Mattis became the most decorated dog in the his-tory of our department, he was only three years old and had been working on the streets for less than a year. Because of the fame of his heroics, his following on social media continued to grow, but I didn't know what his future held. If he was carrying trauma from his fall, it would be selfish of me to make him continue to work and potentially dangerous for him. He still bustled with enthusiasm every morning in anticipation of work, jetting to the hook that held his harness and then—once properly outfitted—waiting by the front door for me to finish my prep for the day. When the door opened a crack, he would nudge it all the way open and sprint to the driver's side of my police SUV so that he could leap in and start the day doing what he loved. But I still wasn't sure that he didn't have trauma from his thirty-foot fall.

During training days, I would intentionally incorporate scenarios that included heights to see whether Mattis had any negative associations or hesitancies. At first, I would do odor searches in close proximity to drops in elevation. I progressed to including a portion where Mattis would have to jump from higher to lower ground to find a source of odor. He showed no signs of hesitation or negative association.

Patriot K9

About eight months after the fall, I brought in a K9 training group that was recommended by my friend Cody for being great at building confidence in working dogs. They were called Patriot K9. Amanda and Jesse, the owners and trainers, were already going to be in the area for another workshop, and they agreed to spend a training day with us. When they pulled up, I could instantly see why Cody liked them. They were passionate and knowledgeable about training dogs. As I described some of the things I wanted to work on, given what Mattis had just been through, we came up with some realistic scenarios that would also benefit all the other dogs and handlers.

Cody, as I have said, is one of the best decoys (guys in the bite suits) that I have ever seen, and he explained that Patriot K9 was also really good at working with a dog and a decoy. The first scenario during our training day involved a building search for a decoy, where the decoy would be noncompliant and fight the dog. As we were getting ready to start, I noticed Amanda putting on the bite suit. It was custom-made and fit her small frame well. It wasn't a particularly thick suit, which meant she would be able to easily move around, but it offered less protection. It was the type of suit pros use because it provides a better image and feel for the dogs, but it means that bites hurt.

I didn't want to insult Amanda, but I was concerned. She was maybe five feet tall and I was pretty sure that if she outweighed Mattis, it was only by a large breakfast. I expressed my concern and told her Mattis was a big dog and he bit really hard, then asked if she really wanted to do this. She smirked—as if this was not the first time someone had underestimated her—and assured me that she would be fine. I heard Jesse chuckle behind me as if he knew something I didn't.

Amanda disappeared into the building and hid. We let the odor settle for a few minutes and then I got Mattis. I hooked him up to his twenty-foot leash, which was typical for long-line building searches because it allowed him to work in front of us at a distance but made sure I maintained control. As we reached the door to the building, I gave announcements to make it realistic for Mattis. "Police K9, make yourself known, or I will send my dog and he will bite you!" No response. "Revier!"

Twenty feet of the leash extended immediately inside the structure (an unoccupied but furnished office building). Mattis worked quickly, following the human odor source to the back of the building and into a server room with rows of computer towers. Mattis went down a row while I stayed back. I soon felt him clamp down on something but heard nothing. I was using the fishing technique described in lesson 7, in which I wait for Mattis to bite and then drag the suspect to my location instead of going to where the bad guy is. It is a much safer approach than just running in.

I was pulling on the line, but it wasn't budging! There was no give. I had used this technique on guys well over 250 pounds with no problem, but I couldn't move Amanda an inch. I finally made the decision to go to her and Mattis. As I made my way to the back of the room, I noticed there was another room behind the row of computer towers. I realized that Mattis must have opened the door on his own and gone into it because I could see the leash was caught in the now closed door and knew Mattis had to be behind that door.

I opened the door, and immediately I was cross body-checked by Amanda, with Mattis dangling from her arm. She flung herself right at me, taking me by surprise. I was also taken aback by the screaming and cursing that erupted from her as she struck me. She held a bottle of water in the hand Mattis hadn't grabbed, and she was dumping it on Mattis and flinging it at me. The pitch at which she was screaming, while alarming, was not unfamiliar. This was the most realistic decoy work I had ever seen; Amanda was re-creating how actual suspects sometimes behaved. This was behavior Mattis had never seen in a decoy, but it was something I had encountered dozens of times on the job. As I stumbled backward from the impact, I couldn't help but smile. Jesse, who had entered with me, was smiling as well. He looked like Mr. Miyagi watching Daniel LaRusso win the All Valley Karate Tournament in *The Karate Kid*.

There was another key way that the K9 Patriot training stood out from other training I had done. Most of the time, when you watch dog-training videos, the way they end the bite scenario is very unrealistic. The handler will tell the decoy to stop fighting the dog, which the decoy complies with by standing as still as possible. The handler stands at the end of the leash and tells the dog to let go. The dog does and then sits. In the real world, it never happens like that. In every deployment I have ever witnessed firsthand or on video, the suspect is flailing, fighting, or complying as quickly as possible to make the bite stop. It never happens when the suspect is still standing or with the handler at the end of the leash. Usually at least the handler but often other cops are also on top of the suspect trying to gain control to end the encounter quickly.

I tried the unrealistic approach first. "Suspect, stop fighting my dog!" The half-full water bottle exploded in my face. I loved this reaction because I hated the unrealistic way bite work is usually done. My smile grew. Amanda was awesome! Since Mattis was locked onto her left arm, I stepped to her right side, placing my right hip behind hers and reaching across her collarbone area. I pushed my hip back, arm forward, and swept her leg, hip-tossing her to the ground. I had Mattis jump over her to flip her to her belly and simulated placing her in cuffs. Finally, Jesse yelled "index"—a term we use in training to signify the end of the scenario.

I gave Mattis his verbal command to release, which he did immediately, and I tossed him his ball. I offered Amanda a hand to help her to her feet and gave her a high five while exclaiming, "That was awesome!" I was so grateful because Amanda poured into my dog in a way he had never been poured into before, at a time when he needed it most. The main purpose of dog training is to build the confidence of the dog so that he believes he can go into any situation and win. You are asking a dog to fearlessly protect his best friend against another human who usually outweighs him by a hundred or more pounds. While Amanda didn't outweigh Mattis by much, she still showed him that he could win in a fight against another that matched or even exceeded his tenacity.

All the teams went through the scenario, and most of the dogs did great. The handlers, however, usually froze when they saw the way Amanda was decoying. It was a great learning experience for all of us, and I really appreciated Amanda and Jesse's realistic approach because it benefited both the dogs *and* the handlers.

Ready for Duty

The final step to make sure Mattis was fully ready to go back to work was taking him to the place where he had leapt over the guardrail. Physically Mattis was healed, but this test would reveal whether he had also healed mentally and emotionally. The sights and smells would trigger any lingering negative memories or associations that might pose as obstacles for him to continue to be my partner. If I'm being honest, it was just as important for me because I had a lingering fear that he would panic when I got him out in a real-life scenario where he would see and smell the adrenaline, fear, and uncertainty. Being a good cop means you have a plan for whatever might happen. If Mattis reacted in a panic, I had no plan. I knew it, and I was terrified.

I hooked Mattis up to a three-foot leash and he hopped down out of the kennel. We walked to the exact spot where he had jumped over the guardrail and fallen thirty feet. I peered over the rail, my right hand on the leash and my left stroking Mattis's head. Mattis put his paws up on the guardrail so he could peer at the same view. I clutched the leash tighter to make sure he couldn't re-create the thirty-foot fall. The weight of my memories rushing back spun me around, and I dropped to the curb, face-to-face with Mattis. The look on Mattis's face as he fell that day was vivid in my mind, but it was very different from the look I saw in front of me now. His eyes were closed, his head lifted high, as he enjoyed the breeze moving through his fur. That day panic and fear had been on his face; now there was happiness and confidence. He lapped at my face, knowing I needed the comfort of a warm, wet tongue raking across my nose and eyelids to give me the strength to get back up off the curb. While I carried trauma from that day (and still do), Mattis showed no signs. He was ready for all that was to come.

Just then, my shoulder mic chirped.

"293, copy, a felony in progress at the mall."

"293, go ahead," I replied.

"Two males attempting to use stolen credit cards at the AT&T store."

"293, en route." I looked at my partner. "Kennel!" I

commanded. He turned, sprinted, and leapt into the back of the SUV, and we were off.

This was a pretty common call we would get. The way it usually plays out is the moment one of the suspects sees a police officer or security officer, he takes off running and a foot chase ensues through the busy mall. Most of the time at least one suspect, but usually both, gets away. Then you just go back to the store and collect as much information as you can for the detectives to follow up on and hopefully track the guys down. It is usually difficult to identify the suspects because they use fake IDs, and if they travel in a car we can identify, it's a rental they fraudulently obtained.

For this call, the best possible outcome would be to arrest both parties on scene. When successful in the past, the important elements were that multiple officers arrive quickly and cover multiple avenues of escape. Time was the most important factor in capturing at least one suspect. This time the store had called it in, so they were just trying to stall the suspects long enough for us to arrive and arrest them. If the suspects were suspicious about how long it was taking, they would just walk away.

I was pretty close to the location, and I had a built-in partner that could help me. The fact that this was a felony in progress meant it met the threshold of being able to use Mattis to apprehend if necessary. The hope, of course, was for a peaceful surrender. One of the greatest assets Mattis brought to the table was that he was—as all police K9s are—a great deterrent. People would see me and think,

Yeah, I can probably outrun that little fella. Or *I can definitely beat up that little guy.* But when they see me with Mattis, their thoughts are very different, and people are usually inclined to be more polite and open to verbal direction. The only times I had the same call and suspects didn't run was because I had a police K9 with me.

I was the first unit to arrive at the mall and knew a back way to get to the AT&T store so the suspects wouldn't see me coming. A mall security guard met me in the hallway as I approached the store and told me they knew the suspects were using an ID and credit card that had been used at a different mall within the hour, and they now knew it was fraudulent. I ran through my priorities as I walked:

1. Apprehend the suspects.
2. Get the fake ID.

The store already had the credit card, so I didn't need to worry about that. This particular store was on a corner on the inside of the mall with exits on both sides. I walked up behind the suspects as they were speaking with a clerk. Mattis was walking briskly by my side, staring at me for direction as I held his three-foot leash in my left hand. Both suspects were dressed in bright orange T-shirts with two reflective stripes running down the front. (I remember thinking, *They aren't going to blend in very well wearing those.*) I saw an ID lying on the table in front of the suspect on the right.

When I was within six feet of both suspects, I said in a cordial tone, "Hey, guys, police here. I need to talk to y'all." They spun around, eyes wide open and mouths agape. Their glances darted between me and Mattis as they decided on a course of action. "Why don't you go ahead and have a seat?" I asked and motioned to the chairs near each of the suspects. The suspect on the left sat quickly. Mattis was on that side, so he locked in on that suspect and stared, waiting for a command or perceived aggression from the suspect. The one on the right started reaching for the ID on the counter.

"Go ahead and leave that there, sir," I said as I dropped Mattis's leash. I could tell he knew he had the suspect on the left covered while I had the one on the right. I approached the suspect on the right to place him in handcuffs since he was not voluntarily complying with my request to sit or leave the ID on the counter.

I reached out with my left hand to take control of his left hand and place the cuffs on him. He swung around with his right hand in a closed fist, reaching toward my head. I stepped to the left as he did and parried the punch past my face and into my shoulder. The momentum turned him toward the exit and he sprinted. After absorbing the blow into my shoulder, I knew my next move was forward as fast as I could go. So as he took off, I almost simultaneously went after him.

About three strides in I had closed enough distance, surprisingly, to dive forward and grab the suspect by the waist. I weigh about 170 pounds but with all my gear closer to

200. Though the suspect looked athletic, it was too much weight for him to bear and he collapsed. The tackle sent us sliding into the walkway just outside the store. As the suspect squirmed in an effort to escape or gain a more favorable position, I slid up to a mounted position on his lower back.

I told the suspect to give me his hands and he screamed, "Get your dog!" I was slightly confused. I turned around to see Mattis latched on to the suspect's right leg. I realized two things very quickly. Mattis had done exactly what he was trained to do without a word from me. The only time Mattis is allowed to make the decision to use force on his own is when there is aggression toward his handler. He saw the punch and realized his duty to protect outweighed watching the other suspect, and he changed focus. The second thing I realized was that I was not as fast as I thought I was. The reason I closed distance so quickly was because a hundred-pound dog had grabbed the suspect's leg just before I went for his waist.

As I looked behind me, I also noticed the other suspect now rapidly approaching in a posture that hinted he was lining up to punt Mattis. Mattis was focused on his task: hold the suspect until told to let go. He also knew that danger was approaching but refused to give up his job. I now became his protector. Still mounted, I drew my Taser and placed the laser sighting on the approaching suspect. He gazed down at the red light on his chest, quickly changed his mind, and took off running into the mall. I called out on the radio that I was in a fight, my dog had been deployed, and one suspect had fled. I gave his description, chuckling slightly as I did because of his bright orange reflective shirt. Other units were arriving right where he was running and they wouldn't be able to miss him. I also told radio to call an ambulance for a dog bite.

Calmly I told the suspect I was on top of to stop fighting and give me his hands, and then I would remove the dog from the bite. He did exactly that. I looked back at Mattis and said, "Mattis, los." He gladly spit out the denim-clad leg and sat waiting for the next command. I told dispatch I had one suspect in custody. A backup unit and firefighters arrived on scene. The backup unit took control of the suspect, and a couple of the firefighters treated his bite wounds. The police units pulling up outside called out on the radio that they had the other suspect in custody.

A couple of firefighters began to play tug with Mattis a few feet away from the suspect he had just apprehended. His tail wagged as he hunched down low and shook his head from side to side, clamping down on the ball with the string. I loved this picture of Mattis; he wasn't stressed, anxious, angry, or fearful. He was just doing what he loved. They scratched his head and he laid his ears back in enjoyment.

As Mattis and the firefighters continued to play, the suspect just looked on, bewildered. He said to me, "I thought those dogs were supposed to be mean. Why he playin' with everybody?"

I responded, "He's just doing his job. He's not mad at you; everything is a fun game for him."

He nodded and said, "I like that."

I took it as a sign of respect for Mattis and appreciation that there was no malice in Mattis's actions (and hopefully mine as well).

As the suspect was taken away, I reflected on this encounter from Mattis's perspective, after he's just been awakened from a nap by the beeps and chatter on the radio:

My best friend is talking. That's good because it usually means we get to go play somewhere.

Deep roar of the engine. That means I have to stabilize myself because of Newton's laws of objects in motion.

Sweet, the blue flashy lights are on; this is when we play the best games.

Quick stop, I need to get my balance. Best Friend's door opens; I hope mine is next.

It is! What game are we going to play?

Short leash hooked up to my flat collar, could be the find-the-smell game.

Best Friend usually doesn't smell as stressed as he is now for that game, and his heart doesn't usually beat as fast as it is now.

We are running! This is probably the protection game!

There are lots of people everywhere. I wonder which is the target?

We are slowing so we must be getting close. Maybe it's these two in front of me; they smell stressed.

Best Friend's tone is not angry, so I shouldn't be either.

Oh, it's definitely these two. I smell the adrenaline and fear. They are huge.

I'll watch this one, Best Friend has the other.

Mine is just scared; I sense something else in the other.

There it is, does Best Friend see it? He's about to get hit, I have to help.

These guys are slow and Best Friend is in the way. I need an angle to grab him.

I can grab his foot if I time it right; I just need an opening.

Got it! And Best Friend timed that well—he jumped right over me.

I got the bottom, you get the top half.

I like when Best Friend jumps in and helps on the running and catching part!

I sense something from the scared-smelling one but it's different now; he's angry and about to kick me.

This may hurt but I am supposed to hold on!

Best Friend barks at him and scares him away. Good bark, Best Friend!

Best Friend says time to let go. I bet he will give me my ball and tell me good boy.

Yep! Chomp, best day ever.

Aww, who are all these people? They seem happy to see me!

Wonder if they want to play with me?

Of course they do!

Two suspects, each outweighing Mattis by at least a hundred pounds, and he had no hesitation or fear. Just confidence, clarity of purpose, and determination. The definition of courage in fur. It was as if Mattis was trying to reassure me he was ready to be back and was teaching me in the process.

Man, I love this dog!

———

As I filled out the mountain of paperwork associated with an arrest with a use of force, Mattis's fearlessness had an impact on me. I've heard that the phrase "Do not be afraid" is in the Bible 365 times. I've never counted, but if it's used that often, it has to mean something. That was the way Mattis lived his life and the way he approached the encounter we had just had. We worked hard in training to build strength so when the real-life situations came, he didn't hesitate. He had trust in me that when I gave him a command, it was in his best interest to obey, so he executed it with enthusiasm. He trusted that even if it went in a way that was unexpected, like a suspect running or another sneaking up behind us, I would fight for him. His actions led me to pray, *God, help me to trust in you like Mattis trusts in me (even as misplaced as that may be). Help me to live as fearless as this amazing dog!*

KEEP YOUR EYES ON WHAT'S MOST IMPORTANT

Lean not on your own understanding.
—PROVERBS 3:5

In January 2019 I received a direct message on Instagram that read:

> Hey there! This is Liz writing. I'm the casting director for America's Greatest K9 and one of your colleagues suggested I reach out to you.

I replied, possibly a little skeptical but intrigued:

> Hello.

She went on:

> I'm not usually on Instagram. If you are interested in finding out more, please email me.

Well, I definitely wanted to find out more, so I sent an email:

> Hi Liz,
> Mark and Mattis from Instagram, here is our email.
> Mark

Liz replied via email and went into detail about the show. She said *America's Greatest K9* was going to be a fun, inspiring, and suspenseful new TV series for a major cable network that would give American viewers a chance to see working dogs and their handlers in action. She said dogs and their handlers from all across the United States would be brought together to compete in a series of real-life challenges. These physical and mental challenges would test their temperament, agility, intelligence, teamwork, strength, obedience, speed, instinct, olfactory skills, and, most of all, the bond between canine and handler.

She had me at "compete." For the past three and a half years I had trained Mattis in a way that was not necessarily customary in the police world. Many departments fear liability, so they isolate dogs as much as they can. They live outside. They interact only with their handlers. They get out of the car only to work. We took another approach. To avoid liability, I followed what I had been taught and seen demonstrated by trainers like Cody, Jeff, Jesse, Amanda, and my dad. Each of those trainers, with their own personal dogs, did not avoid situations that could lead to liability but taught their dogs how they wanted them to behave in those situations. So that's what Mattis and I did, and my department supported it. This would be the opportunity to show a large audience that a levelheaded and social dog could not only compete—he could win.

Liz wanted to set up a Skype call to meet Mattis and me,

and we got it scheduled for the next day. I loved any chance I got to tell stories about Mattis and the amazing things he had done throughout his career. Naturally I told her about his heroics and many awards. She seemed to really like Mattis, and the conversation was easy. At the end of the call she asked me to send her some video clips of Mattis in action.

Thanks to our social media, we had many options to send over. I sent a combination of work videos, both goofy and sentimental. I sent one of Mattis jumping down a six-foot embankment into a muddy creek, exiting the other side, and engaging a decoy. Then I sent a video of Mattis in a pink princess dress and tiara, having a tea party with my four-year-old. The last video was the one of Mattis and me reuniting at the vet after he was released from surgery from his fall. Very different videos, but I thought they showed the dog he was: excellent at his job, tolerant of my shenanigans, and clearly my best friend. The dog has range and was perfect for TV!

Four days passed before I received another email from Liz. She told me I was on to the next round of casting, and the head of the department wanted to jump on a Skype call. The head of the department was inquisitive about Mattis and his accomplishments. It was very similar to the hundreds of questions I had fielded doing public demonstrations over my career, and I loved to talk about Mattis. I genuinely enjoyed the conversation. We hung up and I scratched Mattis's head, and then we waited.

Waiting and Wondering

For two months I heard nothing, crickets, zilch. I started to think maybe they had decided to go in another direction. During that time, the pain I'd been experiencing in my lower abdomen had intensified. A specialist had discovered a slight tear in my abdomen wall and wanted to repair it through surgery. I decided to go ahead with the surgery since I had heard nothing back from the show. The day after I scheduled the surgery, I received another email.

I had been chosen as a finalist from over seven hundred applicants and would be presented to the network for selection. I didn't know exactly how fast the wheels of Hollywood turned, but I wondered if I had just ruined my chances. I called my doctor to see how long the recovery would be for this surgery. He told me that after four weeks of recovery I should be good to get back to physical activities. I kept my fingers crossed that they would be shooting after June in case I ended up being chosen.

Another two months of no updates. The day before my surgery, Liz told me I was in the top seventy-five! She had me fill out release forms, and since I had never actually applied, she had me fill out the application form for what was now being called *America's Top Dog*. She said the series was shooting June 12–26. That put me at exactly four weeks out from my surgery.

The day after my surgery, I received an email with the subject line, "Congrats: It's a GO!" At the time, I was lying on the couch. I pumped my fist and winced in pain from the soreness in my abdomen. I had some people to tell and some phone calls to make. Liz made it clear I could tell family and work but had to keep everything else confidential until the show was ready to promote it.

Throughout the process, I had been in contact with my department about the show and they had been very supportive. They saw the value in highlighting their K9 on a large platform and in potentially winning the cash prize for the department. (If I won, $10,000 would go to our Public Safety Foundation.)

In the email Liz explained the itinerary. Day one, I would fly into Los Angeles and travel to the set's location in Santa Clarita. Day two, I would get to walk the course with Mattis, and they would get wardrobe squared away. Day three would be interviews, B-roll (footage of us posing, walking in slow motion, or otherwise looking cool that the show would use while we were being introduced), and finally the competition. Day four we would fly home.

Over the next few weeks, the producers were working out logistics for the flight and hotel. Since I was recovering from the surgery, I asked if I could come toward the end of the shooting. They scheduled me for June 22–25 on the tenth shoot of the series. I asked what was being shot on the last day, the twenty-sixth. The producers told me that was for the champions competition. They would select some winners from the episodes to come back and compete for the grand prize.

At that time, the protocol to fly with a working dog was to get a letter from your department stating the dog was "on orders" to work and another from your vet with the dog's vaccinations and exact dates the dog would be traveling. On my letters I listed the dates as June 22–26, and I sent copies to the producers as requested. They promptly got back to me and told me I had made a mistake because the last day of my shoot would be on the twenty-fifth. I told them I planned on making the champions episode and figured it would be easier to already have the paperwork ready than make changes at the last minute.

I know that sounds cocky, and maybe it was a little, but I believed with everything in my heart that my dog was that good. I felt like I knew something that no one else did. Mattis was special. This was the time to show it. The producers acquiesced but said they were going to leave the flights and hotel as they were for the time being.

Preparing for the Show

The producers sent over a PowerPoint presentation of what the obstacles the dogs would have to navigate might look like. *America's Top Dog* was now being billed as the wildly popular *American Ninja Warrior* for dogs and handlers. Each episode was going to feature a three-round competition.

The first round would consist of an obstacle course. The PowerPoint showed car obstacles; walls for the dogs to jump over; a slatted bridge, a tower the teams would have to climb with ramps the dogs would have to pull down by jumping up and grabbing a toy; and a water crossing. Five teams would run the course and one would be eliminated in this round.

The second round was an odor challenge. There was a house with multiple rooms inside, and the dogs would have to search items inside the rooms and identify which item had the odor they were trained to find. Once a dog located the item, you would place the item on a pedestal and pull a lever down to see whether the dog was correct. Then you would move to the next room. Two more teams would be eliminated.

The final round was another obstacle course called the Doghouse. Dogs would have to knock down a bridge to enter the Doghouse and jump through a window. Teams would have to navigate a spiderweb of bungee cords before low crawling to a series of boxes. Then they would climb the boxes to get to the second story, where the dogs would have to jump up into ductwork and run through. They would jump down, open two doors, and head to the stairs where the dogs would have to go apprehend a suspect in a bite suit. Dogs would stay on the bite for three seconds, then the handler would call them off the bite from the finish area. Fastest time wins.

I was cleared for full duty one week before I was set to leave for *America's Top Dog*. We prepped for the course as best we could understand from the PowerPoint. In the past, Mattis had avoided water whenever possible but would reluctantly go in if he had to. I had a friend who had a pool for dog dock diving that he let me use for training. Every day after work Mattis and I headed to the pool and got him to the place where he liked the water. I didn't know what kind of doors Mattis was going to have to open, so I taught him on my front door, which had a lever knob, and I taught him how to pull the pantry door open if there was a dish towel tied to it. (In retrospect, this was a horrible idea and the cause of several cereal boxes disappearing.) In the department's K9 training area there were two cars that I taught Mattis to jump on top of and to practice jumping through windows. I worked on calling Mattis off the bite from a distance over and over to the point he would hear me start to call him off and he would let go and run to me. (I knew this wasn't the best for real-life deployments, but for the show it would help my time, and what was the likelihood we would get a real-life deployment before we left for the show?) Mattis was ready!

The day before we left for the show, I was finishing work and passing along information to the oncoming shift supervisors when a call came over the radio of a domestic situation where an intoxicated male was attacking his family with a baseball bat. It was close and I was the only handler on duty that day. Mattis and I were soon en route. Luck had it that two other officers who were both on SWAT arrived just before me. Mattis and I ran into the house, and they briefed me that the male had locked himself in a room and still had the bat with him. Another officer was rendering first aid to the mom because the male had struck her with the bat, and she was bleeding from the head. The suspect wasn't responding to officers when they tried to talk with him and de-escalate the situation. I knew this was a perfect scenario to utilize Mattis.

We came up with a plan. I could have Mattis bark as I gave warnings to try to encourage the suspect to open communication or surrender. Or if need be, Mattis could go in on a long line and I could use the fishing technique to drag the suspect out.

I had an officer run to my vehicle and grab Mattis's ballistic vest. I knew the potential for violence was present, and the vest was designed not only to stop bullets but also to serve as a slash resistant to protect against blunt force trauma. Inside that room was a person we at least knew had a baseball bat and a willingness to use it. He also knew that we were there and where we would enter from.

We stacked up with the shield in front and Mattis and me just behind the shield in case gunfire broke out. I had Mattis bark a little. I then yelled, "All we want to do is talk and get you the help you need." There was no response. I then gave warnings that if he didn't talk to us, we were coming in and he would be bitten by the police K9. Still no response. I gave three more warnings, and we heard nothing. I kicked the door open and sent Mattis into the pitch-black room on a command to locate the suspect and apprehend him. I could hear sniffing and felt the tension on the long line as Mattis moved back and forth. I could tell he jumped up on something, then he clamped down and I heard a loud groan. He had the suspect. I started to pull to drag the suspect out, but the moment I did, Mattis popped off the bite and ran to my side like we had trained for the past week for the TV show. I chuckled at the irony but told Mattis he was doing the wrong thing. "*Fooey* [bad], go stellen!" (I wondered if this would come back to bite me on the show . . . pun intended.) I believe that if he could have, Mattis would have shrugged and thrown his paws up. I knew because of our preparation for the show that I had confused Mattis. I didn't want him to get hurt because he didn't understand I needed him to stay on the bite, not pop off quickly like we had been practicing. I needed to go with him into the room even if it wasn't the most tactically sound move. I am really glad I did.

I hit the light switch on my way into the room and followed right behind Mattis. The other officers were right behind me. As Mattis leapt onto the bed once more and grabbed onto the suspect's leg, the suspect started to swing the baseball bat at Mattis. I dove on top of his arm to prevent the swing, and another officer jumped on top of the suspect with a bulletproof shield across his body. From there we easily took him into custody. I was very impressed with the other two officers' speed of action and how they did not hesitate at all around Mattis. After the mountains of paperwork and some high fives of appreciation to the others on scene, it was off to pack for an early morning flight with Mattis to Los Angeles.

I started thinking about the scenario on the drive to the police station. For weeks I had been focused on preparing for a TV show. I had taught Mattis to pop off the bite at the first sound of my voice or tug on his leash. In an unexpected moment we had to solve a problem we had trained for before. I understood the difference, but Mattis did not. My communication wasn't clear and Mattis hadn't done exactly what I wanted. Tactically speaking, the safest thing for the officers would be if Mattis remained on the first bite and I pulled on the leash and dragged the suspect out to us. But if he had done exactly what I wanted, it was very likely he would have gotten hit with the baseball bat, perhaps multiple times. Mattis would have held on through the hits of the bat, and he would have been injured. I cringed at the thought. I was so grateful it didn't go as I planned.

There were so many lessons I could learn from this incident. Be a clear communicator. Always be willing to adapt to circumstances on the fly. Train for real life. But the one that made the greatest impact is that everything is in God's control. He spoke the universe into existence and knows the beginning and the end. My plans may fail but his will not, and his plans are good plans.

This was the perfect example of Proverbs 3:5–6: "Trust in the LORD with all your heart, and do not lean on your own understanding. In all your ways acknowledge him, and he will make straight your paths" (ESV).

Mattis acted with complete trust in me (definitely misplaced) with all his heart. I had confused him with training for the TV show, but he was able to adapt quickly when I redirected him to respond as he should for real life. Our focus had changed to preparation for the TV show and it had almost cost us. I was so thankful God protected Mattis and the officers on the scene with his plan.

Man, I love this dog!

LET YOUR LIGHT SHINE

Do it all for the glory of God.

—1 CORINTHIANS 10:31

This was my first time traveling with Mattis, so I was a little nervous. It was a four-and-a-half-hour flight and he was a high-drive working dog. Would he be able to sit still? Would he be able to hold it? (You know what I mean.) I knew I wouldn't be able to hold it that long and that he wouldn't fit in the airplane restrooms, so what would I do then? Mattis answered my questions on the flight. Yes, he could sit still. Yes, he could hold it. His attitude was *The flight attendants love me, they can hold my leash as you do what you have to do, and I will guard the door until you come out.* As always, he exceeded my expectations.

On Set

Once I got to the hotel and unpacked, the first priority was to get a double-double at the In-N-Out a block away and then rest. The show would start shooting at 9 p.m. and keep going until about 3 a.m. My internal clock was already thrown off by jet lag.

On day two we were told to meet the vans in front of the hotel to be shuttled to the set. Each K9 team got its own van. We drove about twenty-five minutes into the hills, basically the middle of nowhere, but there were props from other TV shows that had been shot in the same location. We were dropped off by a grouping of trailers with some tents and chairs.

The episode prior to us was shooting their interviews and competition as we were getting wardrobe and an orientation to the course. I was impressed with the entire operation. It reminded me of the logistics in the Marine Corps. There were so many moving parts: transportation, food, lighting, cameras, set construction, clothing, interviews, and more. They had a system down that was pretty efficient.

We walked over to the course where a couple of producers told us we would rotate through the course, spending a few minutes on each element of the first obstacle course, then move to the next obstacle. After that we would walk through the house where the odors would be and then, finally, we would get ten minutes to walk through the Doghouse, the final round of competition.

The time flew by in a whirlwind. I got the chance to interact for the first time with the other competitors on the course. I loved them all. Even though it was a competition, we all were helping each other to make sure the dogs succeeded.

The obstacles in real life were different from what I had pictured from the PowerPoints. The first set of obstacles was a series of cars and vans. They had an entry point toward the back and an exit at the front. On one vehicle they would enter from the trunk, crawl to the front seat, and exit a door;

on another they would jump in the back window and exit through the driver's window; and on yet another they would cross over the top. They switched up the order of the vehicles each night and the entries and exits. We ran it backward and forward to account for the variety.

The next obstacle was the Fire Escape. It was a three-level obstacle you had to reach the top of. The dog would jump up and grab a ball dangling from a string attached to a ramp held in place by magnets. The weight of the dog would bring the ramp down, and the handler would climb to the next level, then they would repeat the process. Once you reached the top, there was a series of steep ramps you could race down to get to the next obstacle. I was impressed by how the set designers created the structure.

Next up was a series of walls the dogs were going to hop over. The first was three feet, then four, and finally five feet. Mattis did these all the time in training at home, so we didn't spend much time on this one.

The next obstacle had you run up onto a platform to a bridge with wood slats between two ropes, which spanned the gap to another platform. The slats were about a foot in width, with about a foot of space in between each slat. Mattis had never encountered anything like this before, and I was nervous he might have some fear. I reluctantly gave him the command to go across the bridge, and he took off like a bolt. Zero fear. I felt a great sense of relief.

Last obstacle of round 1 was the water crossing. The second platform of the bridge led to a pool about ten feet wide and thirty feet long, with a ledge on the entry side and a ramp on the exit side. The left side of the pool had a pathway handlers could walk across to get to the other side. There was a button on a pedestal on the ramp side you would press to stop your time once the dog and handler were both across. Mattis was a little hesitant about jumping in, and once he did, I had to direct him to the ramp. He swam in circles a bit. I realized that this was an area where we could lose time.

We walked over to what they called the Boneyard—the house where the dogs would search for odors. It was a roofless structure built like a maze with wooden pallets. Rooms were constructed to look like bedrooms, living rooms, bathrooms, storage rooms, and locker rooms. Walls could be moved to change up the maze. Producers explained they would hide something in five of the rooms and you would try to get the most finds in five minutes or the best time. The structure was different from most of the places where Mattis and I had conducted searches because it was built with wood pallets and had an open roof. This made it good for cameras to watch the dogs work but meant wind would be blowing through the structure, making it more difficult to find the odors.

The final round was the Doghouse. It was pretty close to what the PowerPoint had shown. Knock down a bridge, get through a bungee rope spiderweb, low crawl, hop on boxes to get to the next level, go through ductwork, open two doors, go down the stairs, and bite the bad guy. This was going to be fun.

I dropped off my shirt and Mattis's harness to get altered

for the show. The shirt was one I had custom-made for the competition. It was gray with Mattis's face over an American flag. I had gotten Mattis a custom-made gray harness and collar. They would both be adorned with *America's Top Dog* patches and a team color.

We were shuttled back to the hotel around 10 p.m. I tried to stay up late because the competition would be shot the following evening from 9 p.m. to around 3 a.m. Jet lag and the busy day made that impossible; I was out. And then, since my body was still on East Coast time, I woke up around 4 a.m. and could not go back to sleep. The next eight hours before we left for set felt like an eternity. I filled them by trying to sleep, playing with Mattis, and scrolling through Instagram. I came across a post from Amanda of Patriot K9 and recognized the pool in the post. It was the pool at the hotel I was staying at! I sent her a direct message—"I know where you are!"—and a picture from the same vantage point. She just sent back a smile emoji. She wasn't on my episode, so I figured maybe it was just an old post. I was so excited she was a part of the show!

Finally, we hopped on the shuttle for set. My mind was racing with excitement. I was so happy to be doing this with Mattis. He was such a special dog, and I couldn't wait to see how he performed. Mattis and I arrived on set and found one of the trailers with our names on a shiny red star. Inside was Mattis's harness and collar and my shirt, now sporting orange patches and fabric.

For the next few hours, we took pictures and shot videos

in different settings. Then there were interviews by the producers. This was the content they would use when the show aired to give our backstory. I retold the story of how Mattis got injured and how proud I was to be in this moment, here, with him. A series of vans showed up on set while we were shooting, and I figured they must be the teams that had been chosen for the champions episode that would shoot the next night. I started counting the vans. Seven. That seemed like a lot. I saw Amanda and her dog Minion, a tiny Shorty Bull, get out of one of the vehicles. We didn't get the chance to talk, but I was excited to see her there. I can't say I was surprised—she's one of the best trainers I have been around. Because of the schedule, I never got to say hey, but I sent her a message on Instagram congratulating her and telling her I was trying to get back for the next day.

After the interviews we had a chance to look at the course one more time. The order of the cars had been changed up, and they made the last wall a crawl-under instead of a jump-over. I knew this would cause a little bit of confusion for Mattis since we had practiced it differently, but I came up with a plan.

I pulled one of the producers aside and asked how many teams were competing in the finale. She told me they were set already with six teams. I felt deflated but I still asked her whether the winner of our show would be on the finale. She said no; logistically it didn't make sense.

I wasn't deflated for long. I knew what I had to do: make them change their minds. I couldn't just win, I had to do something extraordinary so they couldn't say no. That was one of the things I always told the K9 unit back home: "Be so good they have to say yes!"

Round 1

Finally, it was time to shoot round 1. The trailers were parked away from the set so you couldn't see the other teams compete. I could hear cheers from the crowd as each team went. Mattis and I were the last team to go. In extreme situations you can get something called tunnel vision, which is the tendency to focus exclusively on a single goal. In my interviews for the show, they asked me a question that police officers frequently get asked: Why do you do what you do? My answer has always been—and it was also my singular focus now, in the competition—"I want to make God, my wife, my kids, and now my dog proud of who I am, what I do, and how I use what I've been given."

Now as I stood on a platform with spotlights and cameras, surrounded by a crowd, I would have the opportunity to answer the question by my performance over the course of the show. Three short beeps sounded, followed by a long air horn. Go! This was a different environment from what we had practiced in. Mattis could feel my emotions and my focus, and they must have been similar to when we were in tense situations before, when he had to protect me. He shot off like a rocket toward the camera man and was about to latch on. "Mattis, fooey!" I said and pointed at the cars, telling him, *Wrong game, buddy, we are doing this instead.* He understood, made a slight left turn, and jumped, crawled, and slithered his way through the vehicles. It should have been harder for a big dog, but no one told Mattis that. The Car Slalom was finished.

On the first floor of the Fire Escape the lights were making it difficult for Mattis to locate the ball dangling in space. I pointed, he targeted and hit the ball, and the ramp came down quickly due to his weight. The next two levels he knew what he was looking for and pulled down the ramps before I got to them. Down the steep ramps. He was flying; I was trying to keep up. I felt my center of gravity moving forward over my hips and had to grab the handrails to maintain my balance. That was close!

Now to the walls. Mattis was up and over the first two before I could get past the first. He was about to leap the third, but it was a crawl-under now. "Mattis, auf!" (lie down). He locked up as he lowered his body to the ground and sent mulch flying into the wall, stopping just short of the wall. I ran to the other side of the third wall and showed Mattis my hand in the crawl space and told him to come. The space was made for an average-size dog, which Mattis was definitely not. He pushed through and, without a command, ran up the slatted bridge where I had positioned myself once he started crawling under the wall. As he crossed the bridge, I jumped from the elevated platform and sprinted to the next platform that Mattis had already reached.

I had a small set of stairs to climb to get up to the platform, and I could see Mattis on the edge of the platform to the pool, hesitant and looking for a way around. I ran as fast as I could toward the pool. "Mattis, up, up!" I called. He saw me airborne, going headfirst into the water, and his hesitation was gone. We splashed into the pool at the same time. My face grazed the bottom of the pool, and as my head cleared the water, I heard an eruption of cheers from the crowd. Mattis and I climbed the ramp and hit the buzzer on the pedestal.

I didn't know the time to beat, but in that moment, I knew we had accomplished our goal. He was awesome and I just tried to keep up. If we got eliminated, I was still proud.

The sideline reporter came up to us. "Mark, that was incredible. You and Mattis got the fastest time! What were you thinking when you dove?"

"I'm just so proud of him, I wanted him to see I was willing to jump for him like he did for me!"

"Well, you're moving on to the next round!"

We had a break in the action while they set up the cameras for the finds in the Boneyard. I was wet and cold and didn't have a change of clothes. It was June in Southern California, but in the hills at night it got a little chilly. Wardrobe gave me an amazing long, insulated swimmer's jacket, which I was really hoping to keep, and that helped keep me warm. Rounds 1 and 3 were all about energy. Round 2 was about calm focus. While I was on an emotional high, I couldn't feed that into Mattis.

Round 2

One of the executive producers found me on the way back to the trailers and told me they all went absolutely bonkers in the production booth when we dove. But he asked me with a smile not to do that again if I got the chance. That gave me a glimmer of hope, but I needed to focus on the next round.

After about an hour the teams walked down a dark path to the back side of the Boneyard. One at a time they took teams out of sight to the entrance of the house where the crowd was gathered. In the distance you could hear cheering, but you had no idea of the results. When the team finished, they would either sit on the platform if their time was in the top two or be sent back to the trailers if they didn't make the finals. I was last. I stood in the dark with Mattis and a young production assistant for what felt like an eternity. I prayed over and over, *Thank you, God, for letting us be here! Help me recognize what Mattis is trying to tell me.*

They came and got me. Lights, cameras, crowd cheering . . . and in it all I noticed a familiar face. Cody Tallent was in the front row! I thought it was incredibly fitting for him to be there. He had seen the beginning of Mattis's career (back when Mattis was called Cayman), he'd contributed along the way, and now he was here supporting us. (I found out later he was friends with one of the hosts of the show and knew we would be on it.) I gave him a nod and big smile as a giant timer and the crowd counted us down.

Mattis was excited so I calmly gave him a command to

sit up on his hind legs and give me a high five. I whispered, "I love you," right before we got the signal to go. This let Mattis know to be calm and follow my direction. The clock added stress to me, but I didn't want him to feel it. The command was as much for him as it was for me. Having him reach up with his paw and touch my hand brought me comfort. His paws hit the ground and I waved my hand in the direction of the entrance to the house toward odors he could already smell.

The first room was a bedroom. I let Mattis off his leash and let him work independently. It was windy throughout the house and I didn't want to get in his way. He quickly went to an end table on the side of a bed, sat, and stared at the end table. There were two items on the end table, a lamp and a picture frame. I picked up the lamp and realized it was chained to the table. While I was contemplating how to break the chain, Mattis continued to stare at the picture frame. He glanced at me without moving his head as if to say, "Why not grab the one I'm telling you it's in?" I put the lamp down and grabbed the picture frame. I put it on the pedestal and pulled the lever. A green light came and we were on to the next one.

Next we moved into a bathroom. Mattis worked the room and sat by the side of the tub. He was staring at a bar of soap. It didn't make much sense to me, but I grabbed it. Green light. Now the storage room. This was going to be hard. There were dozens of bags on three shelves. Normally I would take them off the shelves and place them all on the ground with space in between so I could tell which one he was alerting to, but I couldn't do that in this case. He worked the bottom shelf. Nothing. At the middle shelf he sat and stared. I needed to know which bag he was staring at, so I gave him a command he had heard before, "Tell me which one, Mattis." He understood, got up on his hind legs, reached over two rolling bags to grasp a backpack, and gave it to me. Green light.

The next stop was a big living room. Wind was whipping through the room. Mattis alerted on the inside wall that there was a large cabinet with dozens of items. He wouldn't commit to one item. I grabbed something and placed it on the pedestal. Red light. I grabbed another. Red light. One more time, red light. I knew I was running out of time. I was stressed. I took a deep breath and thought about what was happening. The wind was blowing from the outside in. It was pushing the odor from the inside of the room to the solid cabinet. I directed Mattis to the coffee table right in front of the cabinet. His head snapped directly toward a book on the coffee table. I snatched it and ran to the pedestal and got the green light.

I knew I had only seconds remaining. I worked my way through the maze to the final room, a locker room. Mattis sniffed the outside perimeter of the room. He went to the center of the room and sat staring at a bag on a bench. As soon as I grabbed it, the buzzer went off. We found only four items, and it was my fault. I should have put the lamp down quicker. I should have thought about how the wind was pushing the odor. I had failed Mattis. I walked out to the stage where two teams were sitting, and the sideline reporter came up to me. "Mark, nice work, you guys got off to a quick start finding four items. You guys are moving on to round three." I was overwhelmed with emotion. My eyes welled up with tears, I smiled, reached down, and gave Mattis a reassuring pat and barely mustered the words, "That's awesome!" through happy tears.

Because Mattis had found the most items in the quickest time, I got to decide the order of the final round. I was going up against Sarah and Fuze, a great team out of a sheriff's office in Texas. In the short time hanging out between interviews and videos, they had become my favorites. Fuze was a smart and beautiful young Belgian Malinois. Sarah was kind, funny, and hardworking. I picked Team Fuze to go first; I would go last.

Round 3

One more round and one more long wait. It was creeping up on 3 a.m. I lay in the trailer while the production crew moved over to the final stage. I listened to music and played with Mattis. Every once in a while I would step out and hang with the other teams. They were all so encouraging to both Sarah and me. Finally, the assistant producers came and got Sarah and took me to the waiting area.

Sarah went to the course, and I stood in the distance and

waited. I could hear the crowd roar and then it got quiet for a few minutes, then there was another roar. A tall, skinny man with a headset waved to Mattis and me to walk his way. He put his hand on my shoulder and told me, "You will walk through this archway and onto the starting platform. Run the course. At the end, if the lights on the house start flashing, you won. If they turn blue, Sarah and Fuze won. All right, questions? No? Go!"

I walked out and stood on the starting platform as the crowd cheered. Three short beeps and then a long one. Go fast! I pointed to the wall. Mattis jumped up and knocked it down. He leapt into the window and weaved through the ropes. I was trying to keep up. Mattis flew up the boxes to the next level and waited for me to get to the top. He ran to the beginning of the cylindrical ducts and jetted through them. He yanked open the doors and flew down the steps. In practice there was no decoy at the end, so Mattis was very excited to see one run out about fifty feet away at the front of the Doghouse. I didn't have to, but I told him to go catch that guy. He flew and latched on. I waited for three seconds and told Mattis to release. Right before we'd left for the show, Mattis remembered me yelling at him for coming off the bite, so he didn't let go right away. He held on for a couple of extra seconds. I yelled, "Mattis, fooey, heel!" He popped off and ran to my side. I knelt down and received him with a hug. He was still focused on the decoy.

I couldn't remember what the producer told me about the lights. Everything was a blank. I saw Sarah stand up and clap and give me a congratulatory nod. Lights were flashing; that meant good news. As I grabbed Mattis tighter, I told him, "Dude, you did it!" I let out a scream and gave a fist pump.

I was finally able to break away from the shoot in the moment right after the victory and find Cody in the front row of the crowd. I gave him a hug and thanked him for his passion and for pouring into us as a team.

I started to walk back to the trailers to pack up when the executive producer from earlier found me and told me, "I guess you're coming back for the champions show tonight! Get some rest!"

Rest didn't come easy. Half the night my mind spilled over with events from the competition that will remain memories for a lifetime. The other half of the night I wondered how I could do better, how I could be faster. I knew the route to improvement was on my side of the leash.

After a sleepless night I crossed paths with Amanda and Minion in front of the hotel waiting for the shuttle. She had spent the previous day with the other competitors who would be on the show that evening. She caught me up on her episode and some of the others. She spoke of one team, Mike and Kai, very highly. She said Mike had been a dog trainer for twenty years and had recently been hired by a department to start their K9 program. She said he was maybe the best protection trainer she knew, and his dog, Kai, was the son of one of his best dogs ever. Apparently, they had the best times in every round throughout the season. For

Amanda, whom I considered to be one of the best trainers, to speak that highly of the team, I knew they must be good.

We made it to set and started the show-day routine. Interviews, video shoots, pictures, production meetings, and a little downtime in between. I got to meet the other teams in the downtime. It was another collection of amazing teams.

The Champions' Round

During the production meetings they told us there were changes to stage 3, the Doghouse. They had added more ropes to the spiderweb and replaced one of the cylindrical ducts with a suspended board. They let us try the new suspended bridge, and the first time across, Mattis fell with a loud thud onto the ground. It was only two feet off the ground, but I didn't want Mattis to get hurt trying it again. I was worried about this obstacle. The producers told us round 2, the Boneyard, had been made more difficult by making the maze more complicated, using smaller odor amounts and a blank room. They also went over the order we would run round 1. They told us it would be according to the times we recorded through the season, slowest first to fastest last. They read out the times for the order. I was fourth fastest. Mike and Kai were the fastest during the entire season, running the course twenty-five seconds faster than I did. Wow! I had work to do.

I realized that this challenge was not going to be easy, and if I wanted to win, I didn't have to be a little bit better but a whole lot better. In my trailer I listened to the lyrics of a song over and over again. It's called "What's Up Danger" by Blackway & Black Caviar. It has a line that says, "Cause I like high chances that I might lose."

I felt like that was the situation I was in, and I loved it. Bring the chaos, bring the doubt. I didn't know how it would end up, but I was psyching myself up to give my absolute best and see how it turned out.

Soon it was my turn, signaled by three short beeps and a long one. Mattis was fast and I pushed myself harder.

"Mark, that was twenty-three seconds faster than your last time. You did it in 1:34!" we were told by the sideline reporter when we finished. I knew it was two seconds slower than Mike and Kai's original time, but I was happy for the improvement. I was in first place, briefly. I was guaranteed a spot in the next round, but as I sat on the platform watching the next teams compete, I was keenly interested.

Next team up set a new season record with a time of 1:29. I was in second. Next team ran into some issues and finished near the bottom. Mike and Kai were up next. This was my first glimpse of them in action. They were smooth and calculated. It was an absolutely blistering pace: 1:10! I was in third.

On to the Boneyard. I was going third out of the five remaining teams. Three short beeps and a long one. The maze was confusing. I was full of stress. I finally found the first room and missed Mattis's behavior changes to find the item. It was taking too long, so we moved on to the next room. I got lost in the maze but finally found the next room. Mattis alerted and I grabbed the wrong item. Another wrong answer. I took a deep breath. Mattis went to the same place. I grabbed the right item. On to the next. Mattis must have known I was out of sorts, so he made it easy in this room. He jumped up on a desk and grabbed the item for me. Green light. I moved into the locker room. Quick find! I went into a blank room. There were no indications and time was running out. I got lost in the maze trying to work my way back to the first room. Time was up.

Cameramen had to show me the way out of the maze. I thought we were going home. At the exit I spoke with the sideline reporter. I told her I was disappointed in my effort but very proud of my dog. She said, "Mark, you found three items faster than the teams before you. You are guaranteed a spot in the final round!" Disappointment turned to hope. I was in first place, briefly. Mike and Kai found all four items. They were awesome. It also meant they got to decide the order of the final round for the remaining three teams. It would go a third team, then us, then Mike and Kai.

Three short beeps and a long one. *Mark, go as fast as you can possibly go. Your dog gives you everything, you owe him the same!* I pushed harder than I can remember pushing at anything. Mattis was still outpacing me. We got to the modified ductwork and he hesitated. He stood on the edge of the duct looking at the board he had fallen from earlier. He placed a paw on it but wouldn't go. He finally tried but fell. I was proud he tried. I lifted him up and carried him to the other side and praised him for his effort. He opened the doors with no problem and we raced down the stairs. The decoy stood across the field and Mattis bolted toward him. I called Mattis to me, but he hesitated. He must have had flashbacks to the night before we traveled to California where I had corrected him for popping off the bite too quickly. He stayed on for ten extra seconds, then ran to my side. I collapsed by his side full of pride but feeling slightly defeated. I had beat the other team and was in first.

Mike and Kai were up. Producers told me what the lights would do if I won, but I couldn't remember. I watched their run from a platform. They were good, but I felt like my pace was faster through the first few obstacles. I think my height gave me an advantage getting through the ropes and the low crawl. Mike was on to the ductwork. Kai froze; he didn't like the suspended board either. The feeling of defeat and doubt started to vanish. The sideline reporter glanced over at me. She knew I was feeling hopeless, and she nodded to encourage me. They took the same penalty I had for not completing the bridge. Then they were down the steps with a beautiful apprehension and good release. The moment before the lights did whatever they did felt like an eternity. Mike reacted to the lights with joy. And I felt a moment of defeat.

Right then I felt incredibly honored to have competed against so many good teams, especially against Mike and

Kai. It was an amazing experience. I told Mike how much I enjoyed competing with him and that he and his amazing dog deserved the victory. He was gracious and humble in victory.

On the flight home I cherished the experience I had with Mattis. Mattis had taught me something in all of this: It was never about winning for him. It was about giving his all and doing it with his best friend. I was proud of him.

Scripture says, "Whatever you do, do it all for the glory of God" (1 Corinthians 10:31). One of my favorite quotes is by Eric Liddell, a Scottish Olympian. He said, "God made me fast, and when I run, I feel His pleasure." His point was God created all of us with certain abilities and has put us in certain jobs or groups. It brings God joy when you use what you have been given for his glory. Mattis had given his all; I had given my all. I was defeated, exhausted, and so very happy. I believe I accomplished what I set out to do: make God, my wife, my kids, and my community proud.

BOAST ABOUT YOUR WEAKNESS

I will boast all the more gladly about my weaknesses, so that Christ's power may rest on me.
—2 CORINTHIANS 12:9

Mattis and I, along with Minion and Amanda, got chosen to go on a media tour with the hosts, Nick White and Curt Menefee, and the sideline reporter, Jamie Little. We flew out to Beverly Hills for some press promos, and later on when the show was about to premiere, we flew to New York and appeared on *Good Morning America* and *Fox and Friends*, and I got to cohost *Live PD*. The whole time I kept thinking, *All because of a dog, all because of this amazing dog!*

Back on the Job

Although we got to experience incredible things and had become more popular on social media than I could have imagined (amassing more than four million followers at the time), Mattis and I were still cops with a job that we loved. So we were soon back to training. As we always did, we trained hard. On the last element of the day, we did a difficult track that was set up through thick woods, then alongside a stream, into the stream, and then a confrontation with a noncompliant decoy at the end. The goal was to mimic a real-life scenario where you not only have to track a fleeing felon but also work with your dog to take him into custody. I was the decoy for the first three dogs on the unit, and then another handler was the decoy for me.

All the guys on the unit knew Mattis was huge, he loved to track fast, and I was small. So when setting up a track for me they would usually include a downhill portion in the track. Mattis would fly down the hill, and there was nothing I could do to slow him down as I held on to his long leash. They got a lot of entertainment out of it, as did I. Sure enough, that's how the track started. They were laughing, I was laughing, and Mattis was working at a full run. We busted through the thick brush to track alongside the stream. Mattis followed the track into the stream and out the other side.

On the bank of the stream there was an incline up to the other side. I could see the decoy about fifty yards away. I gave warnings to surrender, which he did not heed. I unhooked Mattis's leash and whispered, "Stellen." He flew up the incline and had the decoy in no time. I rushed as quickly as I could behind him. Physics is a consistent thing. Measurable. The decoy was six foot six and around 290 pounds. I am literally one foot shorter and 110 pounds lighter than that. What happens when those two bodies in motion collide?

I know the answer. The little one's left ACL explodes. I felt the pop and told the guys I had just blown out my knee so the exercise would stop, and I called Mattis to my side. The pain wasn't bad, but I could feel my knee was unstable. I cautiously walked all the way back to the vehicle, limping ever so slightly, and then drove myself to the hospital.

One of the hardest things for me as I get older is realizing that even though in my head I'm still twenty years old and unbreakable, in my body I am forty-six and fragile. Within the month, I underwent surgery to repair my ACL, but unlike Mattis after his injury, I would be out of full service for six months. When I say I love being a police officer, I genuinely mean it. I love the chaos we are thrown into. I love that we get to step into people's lives during some of the most traumatic situations and hopefully bring peace and light. The injury and recovery meant I would be sitting in an office for a while and would be limited in the amount of participation I could have in the K9 unit. Absolute torture for me!

———

I recovered just in time for the beginning of COVID. Everything slowed, and that included Mattis. I began to notice a slight hitch in his back right leg when he jogged. The vet told me he had gastrocnemius fibrosis, for which there is no treatment. It didn't seem painful but would increasingly limit his mobility. I knew what this meant. The combination of me falling apart, Mattis slowing, and the department becoming wary of the following we were accruing on social media pointed toward my needing to make a big decision. It was time for Mattis to retire. That would mark the end of what I call the best job on the planet for me: being a K9 handler. There was going to be an emptiness I knew I would feel from this point forward.

On March 17, 2021, the city wrote a proclamation thanking Mattis for his service, and the department presented him with a plaque. I was honored and humbled that several followers showed up for the ceremony on the steps of police headquarters. I tried to make it the best day for him. We played the Door Popper Game, where I hide, hit the door popper, and he comes and finds me. We played lots of fetch. Another handler threw on the bite jacket and let Mattis bite him, and finally I got him a pup cup at our favorite coffee shop.

The next day, March 18, was hard. In the morning Mattis ran to his harness as I got ready for work. I sat down on the floor with him and cried. I tried to explain to him that he couldn't come with me. He walked to the front door, confused. I left, and all day I felt empty. Throughout the day I would catch myself saying things like "I'll be right back" to a now empty kennel.

The amazing thing about dogs is the way they show unconditional love. He didn't understand why he couldn't go with me anymore. For months he would continue to wait by his harness in the hopes I would change my mind. Eventually, it changed to him walking me to the top of the stairs and getting scratches before I left (which we still do to this day). But always there was joy when I got home.

What a Gift

Over the next few months I realized what a special gift the time I got to work with a dog was. His absence in my police car taught me one of the most important lessons of all.

As a police officer I see the absolute worst days of people's lives every day I work. When I drive around the city, every street has a memory, and rarely are they good. Robberies, assaults, suffering, and death cast a dark shadow, but having a soft, caring, furry head that would lean on my shoulder eased the burden. Knowing he was listening as I complained about traffic made me feel less frustrated. The way he joyfully and earnestly chased after a ball helped the pain of the moment to fade.

Mattis taught me the profound lesson that strength is born from our vulnerabilities, our reliance on each other, and most of all a perfect Creator. One of the greatest abilities Mattis had wasn't his speed, his tenacity, or even his amazing nose. It was his presence. There were many things that made him special, but the bond we have is the most special.

Working on the K9 unit is the best job in the world. I am so thankful for the time I got to spend working with Mattis and the things God taught me through that amazing pup.

Man, I love this dog!

CONCLUSION

AFTER RETIREMENT

For almost seven years I spent just about every waking moment with Mattis. He is so much more than a dog to me, and I hope you have enjoyed reading about some of his adventures. These adventures—although they are a bit different now—have continued in retirement. Mattis has appeared in several TV series such as Disney's *Just Beyond* and HBO's *Watchmen* and *Black Mafia Family*, music videos with Katie Linendoll, and an upcoming major motion picture. I've written three children's books about Mattis's life and career: *My Dog Mattis*, *My Dog Mattis and the Barefoot Bandits*, and the newly released *K9 Mattis on the Job*. It's not the same as working together every day the way we used to, but getting the chance to introduce so many other people to the amazing things this dog can do helps make his retirement easier.

Many times when a working dog retires, it passes away soon after because its routine—or really, its purpose for living—changes. One of my main goals is to keep Mattis's mind engaged, as it is a key component to extending his life. Before retiring, he got to play games with his best friend every day. I work hard to make sure we continue to play engaging games to keep him young. I'll do things like hide his food or objects with odors he was trained to find often. I'll also put on a bite jacket and let him sink his teeth into it. (He still bites harder than any dog I have gotten bitten by!) And of course, we still make daily content for his social media on Instagram and TikTok and a few videos on YouTube.

Mattis also travels with me to meet and greets, conferences, speaking engagements, and charity events. He thrives in crowds and loves meeting new people, but he's still not the best with dogs other than Storm and Hawk, our slightly less-trained German shepherds in the house.

During the three years of his retirement, Mattis has battled some illnesses. One in particular, gastric dilatation-volvulus (or bloat), almost took him from us, but through all of it he has bounced back like a superhero. He now walks with a limp from the condition that brought him into retirement, but he still loves to play like a puppy.

I've told you about twelve specific lessons I've learned from Mattis, but the lasting lesson I see God teaching me through him is the way he cherishes every moment we are together. The way he lives with his whole heart, loves unconditionally, and remains ever by my side encourages me to do the same as a husband, father, friend, and Christ follower. I hope in reading this book you are encouraged as well.

I am ever grateful for a dog who has always made me look better than I am.

ACKNOWLEDGMENTS

This book is the result of many people being an example in my life—teaching me, giving me resources, and believing in me. When I told others I was writing a book, the first comment was usually, "By yourself!?" The answer is—of course—by no means! Let's put some puzzle pieces together.

I have to thank my dad for instilling a love for dogs and their amazing capabilities. My mom for teaching me to believe I could accomplish anything with a little bit of skill and all the hustle I could possibly muster. My siblings, Kinn, David, and Libby, you are each extraordinary people who are great examples to me.

Erik "Osaki" Larson for the way he serves the K9 community with his art and brings people together with his spirit. It is because of him I met Katie Linendoll. It was a near-miss; she had another dog booked for her music video, and I wasn't sure I wanted to drive to Nashville on short notice. But it was a divine appointment that we would meet and become friends. She fell in love with Mattis and saw something in me. Without Katie this book would have never happened.

Katie connected me with a literary agent because I wanted to write another children's book (after self-publishing two). Lisa Jackson with Alive Literary Agency saw potential in me to tell our story to a broader audience. She listened and encouraged, and then she pitched not only another children's book about Mattis but also this book.

Thomas Nelson for taking a chance on a first-time author without a manuscript. I am truly humbled and grateful that you did. Your team has been amazing, and the process has been invigorating. A special thanks to Brigitta Nortker who helped this uneducated, crayon-eating, former marine embrace the Oxford comma. You earned your keep as an editor on this one, and I am so thankful for you! The editing process was a blast because of you.

Mattis, obviously, because he is the goodest boi and the whole book is about him, but he can't read any of it. My kids, Makenna, Cayden, and Harper, who make me want to be a better dad every day. Part of the journey I've chosen for my life is to be a good example for my kids, point them toward Jesus, and hope they may see some of God's love in me.

My wife, Tamara! She is the most amazing person I have ever met. She relentlessly loves, serves, and gives of herself. She is beautiful on the inside and out. She tolerates all my shenanigans and shakes her head with a smile. There is no way she knew what she was getting into when she said yes to me in 2001, but now she's locked into it! She is way out of my league, and I hope she never realizes that.

Finally, all the people that smashed a Follow button on social media or bought my children's books. I wanted to bring people together with our story when the world seemed more divided than ever, and you showed me that the majority of people wanted the same. This is because of you and for you!

ABOUT THE AUTHOR

Sergeant Mark Tappan shares a special bond with his K9 partner Mattis, one of the most decorated police K9s of all time. He knows that true success is built on relationships—with friends and family, the communities we're in, and the dogs beside us. He learned his canine-training skills from his father, who trained Labrador retrievers. Mark often talks about how his determination and competitive drive set him up well for his careers as a marine, a youth pastor, and now a sergeant in the Alpharetta Police Department. While Mark has trained many dogs in his tenure as an officer, he believes Mattis is the best.

Can't get enough of Mattis?